Obama's

The

DE-CONSTRUCTING

of

AMERIKA

essays

by Charles E. Miller

Order this book online at www.trafford.com
or email orders@trafford.com

Most Trafford titles are also available at major online book retailers.

Printed in the United States of America.

ISBN: 978-1-4269-9479-1 (sc)

Library of Congress Control Number: 2011916356

Trafford rev. 09/16/2011

 www.trafford.com

North America & international
toll-free: 1 888 232 4444 (USA & Canada)
phone: 250 383 6864 ♦ fax: 812 355 4082

Preface

In the two and a half years that President Obma has been in office, he is persoanally responsible for numerous violations of his power and authority under the Constitution, a debt into the trilliosn which the people will never payoff, great numbers of unemployed because he has vir;tuallydestroyed the consumer base with his taxes and his spending, and growing numbers of citizens dependent upon the largese ofthe Federal Government's entitlements. Not the least of his boondoggl pieces of egislation is Obmacare, a leviathan health care bill that will drain one fifth of the natilon's economuy Barack Obama is a radicdal and a Marxist idealogue .

I have culled my e- mail Letters to a Citizen composed over two ad a half years the following commentary essays on Obama;s performance in office. Also, I have attached postscripts to append thoughts and comments germane to that prticular letter.

This collctin of essays is my crfitique of the most radical Presi dent we have ever empowered in this nation's history! He does not work alone, howeer; he has his advisors, new czars and radical leftist members in Congress. Many Liberals have fallen into lockstep with Obama. America is on the verge of bankrupcy because of Barack Obama, specifically because of his wastrel, incompetent and unchecked policies of spending, borrowing from our enemy, Communist Red China. Obama ils deluded to beliee that hecan create jobs by throwing good money after bad and th...not on borrowed moneybut on goods and services energied andcreated by business left to use ilts profits for growth, not for Federal seizure. . Trillions in loans will last only so long and we still do not know ltheir destilnation! His tax policies are stripping the wealth of this country from the hands of those who create that wealth, the American people whose free market system utilies profits for growth, not for Federal acuisition. May Almlighty God preserve and guide this nation henceforth! Our government is in the hands of demonic powers.

PREFACE TO ESSAYS

There is a temporal quality to these essays, which means their substance is transient, related to the present Obama Administration. However, embeded in their thought are assurances of this nation's future and affirmation of the provisions, protections and constraints of the US Coinstitution. Therefore, I put them into print. It is always imperative that loyalists to this nation speak out, and I presume to have done so with these essays. They represent the resistance thinking of millions of Americans, another reason I proceeded wth their publication. They also constitute an implied warning against power-mongers who wish to control the lives of a free people, beyondf the protection and care of n omnipotent God, in whom our Founders believed and in whom they placed their trust in to annoint their laborsin Philadelphia in 1789. I write, then with some perspective on history and insight into the problems that these essays refer to and attempt to correct. Freedom without God is anarchy because human justice supposes the secular control of fainess, which is always flawed by human reasoning.

Man is fallible, even the most tyannical leaders commit errors mortal to the continuation of a great document, the fundamental law of a nation of three hundred million people, and the guardian of our hopes and visions for the future. This vision supposes a just people rather than a just State--the latter when man-centered being a liberal, Leftist premise--which inevitably presents the control of freedom by the introduction of laws of fairness. We are a nation of laws, and thus I write to indicate how the present tyranny, leading us in the wrong di rection toward socialst controls, presumes to address our laws while at the same time isolating them with impunity and spending generations to come into bankrupcy on the theory that spending by the State liberates business enterprise . However, as experience proves, the liberation must come by way of expansion of the consumer base. The finest products and services in the world are of little value if the people lack the money to purchase them. Hiring more employees does not put money into the pockets of customers. For if that money comes from the Govenment, it is limited by the terms of the loan. Once gone, it is gone.

I have no compassion for the Tyrant who, as I have indicated, has taken over the fundamentl law as if it were his instrument of personal regulatory opinion instead of law. And so he proceeds to the ultimate destruction of this great nation by the substitution of an alien ideology to replace our protective Constittion and our system of free enterprise. Insofar as these essays represent one citizen's rebellion against the tyrannical Central Government nowadays in America, I think they have been worth my efforts as one man's scrutiny of laws that he has lived under for many turbulent years. I have earned the right to rebuke the Tyrant. I have learned that First Amendment right by my reading of our Founders' work. Thus I present my rebellion in the form of these controversial essays, and I shall do lthe same with my vote.

FROM THE BULLY PULPIT

THLETYLRANNY OF FAIRNESS

Citizen.

Under socialist government, there must be no self linterest, no contest of equivalency, no ligitation , under amendmentVII, of discourse on differences...all are qequal. ILn ATere must be no self linterest, no denlegration of the other party, no losers.

Socialism abridges the law; of conracts by removing parity, a thing of value forin ecchange for another thing of value.This basis' for a civil contract is destructive of the Socialist dicta of equivalence pf all contracts, their measure of w ealthbeing the sameand withut controversy,in moot negotiations sat comon law. The element of equivalence and therefore of fraud ilsalways present in a Socialist agreement b ecause of this fictitious equi;valency. In thle Sociaist mind there is no real tradeoff, only a false parity. b ecause thle Government contlrols the value of all material things, goods andservices.   Therefore, contedtlng litigation ny propey-owners, an illusion in view ofState absolute ownershlip, is unacceptable u n a State civil court, wlith or with a 8out a jury   In other words, discursive negotiations are scorned in a Socialist environment. because they impoly capitialist ownership and therefore are anti-State. Private property is made to be a sham in a Statist country, an illusion to mollify old hangers-on from Capitialist days. The citizen,in other words, cannot sue to collect a judgement, becaue such awards are contary t State morallity of fairness.   Any consignment that transgresses that dictum i s trans skirted or abolished by the Department of Justice. It ;makes the individual infeior to the Syate lin rights and powers of conrol. Ever watchful to protect lits rilghts, Je o;s mp ;pmger tje spirce pf STate. prGpverm,emta; . power/ The State cannot eilter toleratd the immoralt and often umnethical ransgression of oyd [pert nu contoversial litigation. Justice is the essence of a heartfelt ruling by the Magisrate.   And so it should be in any litigous disagreement. The disagreement is human; the soluton is virtuous and godly,   thle ruling is fair because the STate deems silt to be so.

Preslident Obamas selection of Sotomayor and K agalto the Supreme Court will meet the demands of his new Amerika. Kagan will rule on the conept of a clhangeable Constitution, wlithot Amendment and with Col;urtrulings only. otomayor wil base her rulings on thedoctrilne of Statilst regulation, which meets no contest and is therefore pren even ifancillatsorytothe Constiltution, and begs to be moral iln the summary. Both appoointees are statists, the reasonthat Obama chose them tof illt hevacancies left by Breyer and ....The Amerilcan people can expect mroe legislation to come from theench, tangential tot heConstitution, a living and breathing document...a otallyr omantic and urnealistic notion of our fundamental law! By using theCourt to reah an opinion, a personal socialist opinin, om a subject of controversysthat involves land, proerty, natural rights, the Executive assu;;ed uto himself a rlight hand use of the Ssupreme Cout toe xecute his visionfor a Socialist America, for to him the old ways under theConstilution are crafty, selfish, designed to uphld slaveryand the world of self appointed old meniln theConstiltutional deliberations iln Philadelphia.

We shl see. Qw obama assumes mor eand more thaspect of adictator, garbing himself in therobes sof atyrant, control of the Supreme Corut, amssive borrowing debt, ancillary apojtees wlith hiddlen powers and costs to the people, thousands of pages of regulations that emplyhis favorite trial attorne;ys and the major stumblinblock Oama care...these dilsilngen;uous developents and selizures of pwoer , while theyadorn hisgrace for another yer and a half, annot remain because the Ame;rlican people have a history he overlooks t his convenience. The same pair of hands that guided the plow that broke the plainswil be behindconservative tillage of the peoples potential. The same will, the same taking of rilskwill animate new projects that willrecover from Washington the basis power o ilndividual lierty and the promises inthe Declaration of Independence...life , libertyand the ursusit of pohapilness. Theliberals, efists and Marxilsts have a surprise ins tore for them in their ceasequest to remsake America into the image of amilsanthrope named Marx,who watched withalien disgust, anger and nvythearistocracypass himdaily as he sat inthat Lndon library. His Manifeto isfor another age, another society. We have no aristocracyfor Obama to disenthrone, thltough he attempts ot impoly that CEOs of corprationsare that aristocracy. He is a fool. \\

In order to achie ve his end result a Socialst State, Barack Obama must mis characterie the American people. Hwe pimputes to them the character ofthieves! Theyhave stolen from the rest of theworld: that theft explains their esceptional society of obvious opulentce compared to the impoversished regions in the world. He cannot nor can heshow, name one country wthat as sutained fatal looes, leqadilngto widespread pvoerty, that has suffered that condition from America;s theft of her wealth. Tht lie is an insult to the American who labor, livent, plan and achev eunder our system of Constiltutional govermment. To achieve i sSocialist State, Obama must: (1) ruinthe value of thedollar by printing money; (2) put the people into such indetednessthey can never recoer, ;trillios of debt; (3) Destroythe constitution as a viable and controling document of basic law; (4) demeanthe amerlican eople as hieves, limopugn their characgter; (5) create a societys entitleents upomnwhichthe people, slowly deprived of theirill gottengains, cometodepend for their verysussistence; (6) coneive of progress as ilncreasing growth of the FEderal government. (7) Haingimuted th character os gthives to the people, the State now assumes themantle of savior, forgivingthe people intheir new state of abject povty and therefor eecoming the sosurce of goodness, moral condut, benevolent compassion and all forgilveness, lina word, God. The State then becomes the ogject for worship by the people in their blind, abject dependence upon the Central Governme;nt, now no longer considered a government but, isnt4ead, a regime of power hundreyy lesser yrants wlith their own litle duchies of rule, a Medileval oligarchy once again. Do ot the people see how etrogressive and unethical andlmmoral this return tos the Middle AGes canvbecome. Transformed , to b sure, bsut accordling to the Secondlaws of thermo dyna;mics, ;linto a nation of less power,

opulence, brillant dilsplay, wealth, comity, comfort aand security, a cheap;e;;ning of the soul
of Aerilca by this one man whose vision lis pathetically out oftouch wliths the real America.
He lives ilna political fantasy world of make believe abou our people, our history, our rights
and out ambiion. When he talks about "jobs: he lies. That is a propaganda hot word that
attracts the people, who need jobs, to a polity that cannot work. It bears repeatilng:
thegovernmentc annot spendmoneyto creat wealth and propserity. That is illusory wealth,
federal workers...without toching the economyand theresl cause, the destuction of the
consumer base by trillions in taxes and p[a[er facproes spf regulations to conrol a stupid
people. illt ils hard or a n ilndependent people to understand that perverse ,mentality and
desire; buthey are there, vilsible lin barack HusseinObma.

TSGE CRILSIS, by Chrles E. Miller

POSTSCRIPT. Failrsness has another aspect, other than equivalency, that few
politicians touch uponand evenfewer conervative-inded ocmmenttors explre. That aspect is
not that there can be no wlners since that a lost woul suffer the discrase of losing and that
would prove tovbe "unfair.: What the philosoph of STatilst control does to the humanwill to
succeed, to acheive. lWlithothose goalsremoved, abject mediocrityb ecomes the norm, thef
ashion for the medicrity seen alla bout one lin this new Age of Statilst control.
IL;ndividualtalent ils swept aside,d ismissed as not relative to thed ayand age or to the
concepts of an eual society of all achievers, no dilscrimination between good andbad, trueand
false, beauiful and ugly. The extilngushing of the wil to achiev e is a hall amrk of the Statist
sciety. Ahileve? To towhat end, tow hat purpose, for what reason.> Indeed, the very
consept of 28thcenturyenlightment, the use of reason to resoslv lifes problems , wil have
beenextinguished. The Central Governmen wislldo thereasoning, theree ils no longer
anyresosnfor menreason outtheir lives, their risks,their usefulness to thestate...Iwas goin tos
ay inestments. ILnvestments are scorned, theveryword ils opprobrious slince it implies the
possession of Capital. Mediocrlitywillb eomethe acceptable presentation of any remainign
talents; let no mans worksupercede that of another in quyality,b auty, character or intent.
Medicrity wil rule all endeavors,s fromt he school classroom the theStateowned companies of
controlled production. Mediocrity...yetwo will eventuallyb able to saythat this object sor
work or process if mediocre, when there no loner exist any outstanding works by which to
copare the efforts of State drugdges.   ?Medilocrlity will produce hapoiiness,whateve hlat
word willcome to means...slothful conentment wlithentitlements, all of lifes problems
resolved by the State which, rememvb;er now, was once the eceptionalist nation of American
society that stood aout amidst therest of the impoverished world, Mister Obama. Your
investment lin Cheese stock will furnish us wilth blue llights to light our way in a darkened
world, nest pas?

TRIAL OF JIHADIST FIVE

Citizen.

The American Courts are intended for US citzens. The Federal Couts are not a Global or an International Court, although the world will now accuse the US of redefining justice of a trial by the Hague panel of three ustices. .The unusual civilian trial is to seek and covet the approval of the world for his, Obama's, opiionated sense of fair jutice. Afer all, our enemies have the same rights as our civilian criminals. They shouldbe read their Miranda rights. The Nazis tried at Nuremburg...were they read their Miranda rights? Be confident that the arrangement is to justify the Nobel Peace Prize. I mean, atfer all.....a Military Tribunal would constitute an unfair justice. Such a trial would prove divisive. His Marxist ideology abhors abosolutes like the convictions of Pariots. For Barack Hussein Oblama, a Military Tribunal would be unfair to the prisoners, the 200 batlefield combtttants! When shooting an enemy in time ofwar becomes murder of a civilian from another coutry, that isthe end of war.   President Obama cannot remoe evil from the world; only the Lord God, not Allah, can do that at His Second C oming. So slack off, Mr. President. You cannot change human nature or the fluctuations of history's enmities between nation. Just w hy hy are these five enemy combattants, as it ils proposed, to be tried in a citizen court under laws of procedure and adjudication that protect US citizens? Willthley also not tried under rules of sustantive evidence for which there are no precedents in civilian courts, unless an armed insurrection can be classified as warfare. WHy are they not being tried in a Military tribunal under the laws of nations that govern prisoners of war? They are POWs, captured and held at Gitmo to protect the troops in he field and to protect Continental Us from another similar 9/11 terrorisgt attack. They are not civilian criminals.Their cause of a action is the justification for militaryengagement, provoked or unprovoked, discrilminatory or non-discrilminatory, purpose, anticipated and directed. Rules of engagement and,therefore, causes of action control these matters.

They will lose their status as prisoners of war!   The pesumption of innocence will be applied to all of them. The Federal ccourt will morp these five dangerous war combatants nto "civilian citizens, innocnt persons of interest, suspected of potential acts of terror, the destruction of another twin towers and all persons therein. Yet they are innocent. How canthis be? Explainthecontradition.   By this transgression of common law, we have reached a state of jurisprudential anarchy! As forbiddenby Sharia lw, there will e a jury...of whom? Our frinedly field combattants? US troops? New York citizens? Absurd! The farce grows more involved..

The politically-correct Left and largely Demcrat attitude is preparing to corrupt the American judicial system with the approval of our President and the liberal Congress. This ambivalence has one purpose: --to blurr the distincntions between a common-law criminal motivated by a crime for gain and a terrorist motivated by an ideology to kill for Allah and paradise. The upshot of the latter, sustained by Attorney General Eric ;Holder, whether he admits it or not , is that there can no longer be a Constitutional system of civililan protection-- for civilians are the same as military criminals-- and that all the Attorney General needs to do is to place a terrorist under civilian apprehension, including refined interrogationt techniques. That blending, confusion, similarity of of trial philosophies and procedures for Civilian and military criminals is a demonstration of the Admiistration's lack of moral discernment. Een now, Tea PartyPatriots are geing called"terrorists."

The enthusiasts for such an ironic and "romantic" blending of civilian and military justice have not the wisdom of undersnding that there are significant differences between a common-law criminal trial and a miliary trial for Johadists. At Nuremberg, twenty eminent scientists and doctors were idealogues, Nazi idealogue practicioners of crimes against Nazi enemies, chiefly the Jews, andalso homosexuals and the physically handicapped. . Today, the battlefileld venue raises the question of convicting evidence. Even concerning the five to be tried, the question of evidence becomes moot with the change in venue from Gitmo to a Lower Mamnhattan Federal courthouse. Hearsay evidence, stricken down in a common-law court, can play significant part in this trial, if it occurts. (Hersay is "he said" e vidence.) Will the evidence show an intent for a coordinated four-prong arial attack on America be sufficient evidence to convict?. Rememer: these five prisoners will be sitting there presumed to be innocent of the crimines they are charged with. Count on it: the Prosecution willread passages from the Koran thatexhalt relligousretribution against non0believers. Note: battlefield killingv of the American enemy will require substantive i.e. tangible proof. Wilthout that evidence, it is quite possible that the civilian court can and will exonerate the battlefield combattants, they having proved themselves the enemies of the Unted Sstates for having gaged in armed warfare agaist American troops.

Is religion or is batlefield killing on trial? oris the latter murder for whichuslimscannot e condemned and/or tried in a foreign court apart from Sharia law? Thee questions make thetrasfer a stickymtter for any courtgin Western society. Are these five men actually prisoners of war or are theyreligious fanatics acting out Koran laws agaisnt The Great Satan, the Unigted States qne therefore unjustly imprisoned? Are they, in fact, either triable in a civlian coutt under our laws? What specific law? Or, does a civilian target rule out the fomer cause of action--religion? If the latter is so--they are civilians-- then the five are not the"usual " POW's. Therefore, why are they even being held? They are held because they plotted, it is alleged, to murder nnocen Americans as religious targets. they, the Gitmo five, therefore, become terrorists after the fact of their alleged inocence. The fuestiojn tstill remains in a civiliancourt: a "terrorist" is astate of being. Where is the crimeof ach prisoner, and its evidene thereof?

I think this trial will result in a new code of laws that overturn the prosecution of combattants who are terrorists, to be sure, who serve in the army of a religious ideologyy carried to the extreme of death to non-believers!.This trial will now, however, be a trial of the

Islam religion. The trial will concern what the five actually did, when they conspired to bring down down the twin towers, motivated by their religion. They were imprisoned at Gitmo t with the other 200 because the results were the same...kill the satanic Ameicans.

It i my opinion as a US citizen that laws that pertain to acts of espionage should include the accused perpetrator's plans to blow up Amricans in four venues , one inferred. Acts of expionage are acts of war , yhe recogniion that a state of war now exits beween the Jihadists and the American nation (American Capitalist-secular free society versus a Johadist one-world Islamic Government). Therefore the Jihdists can be tried as enemy war-combattants. The charge of criminal-conduct can be brought, I think, on the grounds and evidence of

(1) the size, measure and scope of the killing, 3,000 murders of non-parcipatory innocent civilians; and

(2) the precogniion of the consequences of mass killing as murder of civilians. All wars down through human history have ivolved the killing of innocent civilians.

(3) the long preparation e.g. flight shools prccedent to the mass murders;

(4) the tentative and transitional nature of the 3,000 murders that precede, antipate and futther the cause of Jihadism,and its offshoot , Hammas, the world over. This experimental nature converts what are simply war- time agents of religious espionage into crimials with the intent to convert, to change America into a Muslim natuion. The first step is to kill all the infidels of The Great Satan. It is the act of mass kiling of innocent Americans that is on trial, not the relaigious motivation. The latrter will be the Defense thrust ...to prove that the entire Afghanistan and Iraq war is an attack on a religion, begun by George Bush. As a retaliation, even in war, espinage is a fair strategy.   Their guilt, even as agents of a foreign religion, will obstruc their remoal from Gitmo, even totheir own countriesd where they can again engage in combat against America.

If they are not imprisoned until death--at an even greater taxpayer expense,--but they are released into the general populace after we have forgotten the trial , you can blame Barack Obama, his Chief of Staff Emanuel Rohm,, his Attorney General Eric Holder, and all the other liberals of the Congress --Pelosi and Reid most noteworthy--who are gluttonous for power and care little if at all about the people. Their word lis no longer credible.

This trial will obscure and blurr the lines between civilian and military justice, and acts of violence. between a crime and a combat attack. The Trade Center , Pentagon and Pennsylvania field tragedies were terrorist, read a "military," acts , identifiable by their concerted purpose to kill the reat Satan people, as soldiers for Allah...and concealed by the lack of military uniforms, they did no escape detection but became captives by the rules of combat warfare acknowledged by all nations.

You must have recourse to Sharia law in order to understand the motive behind the twin-tower and Pentagon attacks. In effect, our American laws will have to impugn Sharia law. by this trial. Court-appoined Defense will have to deflect that condemnation. As for the Proscution, failure by the Defense to present to the jury convicting evidencet, the judge--sealcted from "the wheel," will release the prisoners with the "PC feelings" statement that they have served enough time behind bars and therefore they "deserve" to be freed. . (Feel for them!) With the feminization of the adminisration and the money-for-power corruption of the Congress and the dumbed-down abdication of the media to truthfully critique government, this release outcome is a possibility.

he wisdom of discernment of universal truths is lacking all around. For example:--he who submits to his enemy invites attack to fix control and exploit weakness.

Anotherexample:--Wisdom does not come from the barrel of a gun. It comes from a discerning consciences infomed by the God of our pilgrim Forefathers. Arm Your homes.

In a proposed clivilian trial, uch defense information will be revealed, not just refined intgerrogation techniques. The potential exists that with the lack oif sufficient convicting evidence, as criminals, the prisoners will be released.

Without discovery of evidence to convict,--videos of the battlefield engagements is hearsay and speculative--the prisoners , unless the judge intervenes, will sue for being forced to testify agaainst themselves, endure an un-Constitutional length of encarceration, deprived of right to call witnesses to defend, and malatreated with cruel and unusual punish;ments such as wateroarding. They will use thearguments sof civilian prisoners, not ;military..

It has been rightly pointed out that these civiian trials of war criminals in Lower Manhattan--instead of in a military tribunal--will provide a forum for the liberal left to indict George Bush, the CIA and the refined interroationt techniques i.e. waterboarding used to extract information from Sheik Mohammad.. (Can fear of drowning be construed as torture--instead of a threat or escruciating pain or bloodletting? Eminent specialists on torture will be summoned to testify, psyciatrists, prison guards, pastors , past warime prisonersd , the prisoners themselves.) Thequestion remains: is wterboardingsbjecgtive "torgture" omust torture be physical to so define it?

The trial will be long and costly., perhaps three to four years at a great expense to taxpayers. The prostitution of journalist reporting wil go on and on. Selctive camera workwill create "sides."

The Defense will usurp the Consitutional protections intended for citizens of the United States.. Obama, you can be certain, is behind this transfer of site to New York. Eric Holder ,sounding legitimate but ambitious for power and historical recognition, is pushing the transfer.

All who care little about the integrity of this great nation are campaigning for the move. Obama's Soviet-style AGITPROP is jpatently desructive of America;s prestige.. The change in trial site is political, ill-concelved, dangerous and lacks the empowerment and acceptance of the Congress. In a word, the decision is a stupid decision. Marxism is a stupid and unwokable philosophy. Obama will appoint his 40th Czar! - -Keeper Saffron Dualome--Czar of the Prisoners

Jury selection will be long and complex and distrustful by both sides and the American people. Cameras will be allowed with a teleprompter for Barack Obama. It will be a gaudy show of power, intrigue, misrsust, cajolery, refined sentiments of compassion and a sickly Obamaese appeasement before the world...ye showing the world our strict attetion to rules of procedure.

The trial will stir up a windfall of propraganda for the enemy and aginst The Great Satan, supported by the Little Satan Israel--our enemies , emboldened further by our cowardly over-attention to prisoner rights. Caesar's circus, for sure, a comedy of errors, a semantic fallout of linguistic misinterpreations, a mega-stage for a blundering justice in a compassionate nation,.

Our enemies will perceive the trial as an illusion of truth that masks deceit for the American people.while behind the scenes the little smiling dictator is contriving other schemes to further bond the people to an inept liberty-snuffing government.

What if the jury is a hung jury? Comes a counter-suit. What if the Defense pleads insanity?. How much will be the pay-off by Obama to trial lawyers, his srongest campaign supporters...which is, I suspect, a chief reason for a civlian trial (and the reason there is no tort reform in the Healthcare bills).

Where th reainign 200 prisoners willbe housed is another issue. W Notice, the plan is to "House" them, not to "imprison"them. Treat hese Jihadists, who want to blow up Americans with kid gloves, like ordinary citizens inconvenienced by prisonment. Introduce them to Janet Napolitiano,their willd-eyed Gatekeeper. . Give them creature comforts, oriented to Mecca prayer ru\gs, cell phones to converse with Allah and better-than-citizen medical care. Anything short of these creature conforts would be maltreatment bordering on torture. Anything shy of thse amnities would conststitute the denial of prisoner rights. Obama prompt will be prompt to chose ,by legislative sanction (Ten Amenments) a Czar for Prisoner Rights.

THE CRISIS, by Charles E.Miller 11-13-09 11-19-09

POSTSCRIPT: Evident to many observersils the attempt bylthe Obama Adminisration to victimize the Jihadists, intheface of their long iprisonment. Tha would beaccomplished by the deletion of the military violence fromtheir recrds and, insead, place hemon before the court as civilian criminals, eventhough involved in espionage, for which they can be tried under the rules of evidence consistent witha civilian trial. As victims of the "American system of jusice" they could e releaed back into their owncontries, ahving spent timealready at Gitmo for theiralleged mutiple crilmes. Exonerated as vlictms iln a cilviliancourt, O bama's "conscience" for the men would be vidicated, as would his Muslim background. He would achieve this result without the intervention, or eventhe consideration, of Shria whiich would grant criminal amnesty i.e. forgiveness, exoneration for the accused five Jihadists.

REFORM AMERICA, CENSURE HER FRIENDS,
FLATTER HER ENEMIES

Citizen

The gang of pirates from Obama on down through Greasy Axelrod, Rahm 1 & 2, Sanctus Sanctorum Pelosi, Bendable Reid, Treasury Feinstein, Tenth-Round Boxer, More Light, Waxman, Cash Stenosis Geitner, All's Well Napolitano, Eric (the bull) Holder, Cyclist Kerry, Barnacle Frank, Cris-cross Dodd, Swastica Durbin, Frog- in-his-Throat Leahy...this gang of looped up radical detestables .is determined to trash American history and the most human, inventive and deployable system pf medical care ever known to Western civilization. In its place these Lilliputians will substitute the pathetic, impractical, clumsy and corrupt system invented by a social outcast, Karl Marx in a London Library. Now it's up to the people to drg these gangsters out onto Feedom s treet by their money-belts when next we ote for a change i the Presidency. t.

The Obamacare plan lacks Constiutional restraints, oversight, is subject to manpulation for fraud that rips off the taxpayers, fattens the trial lawyers and that will lead our medical care to mediocrity, incompetence, ongoing lawsuits, massive confusion of data, mistakes in judgement and partial care, and virtual total destruction, of a working healthcare that will become totally inadquate, as in "advanced" Europe.

Do you admire European medicine? Go there for your heart surgery. You may die there! It is sad, is it not, that our State Department Head Hillary Clinton cherishes Marx's memory! Marxism is weak, inadequate, impractical, fraudulent and wrong for free men, if not for European Medieval serfdom. Give one example of its success of "advanced Marxist care" Western history.

You want to be a Swede or a Dane? Go. You'll wait two years for a total hip replacement, and then the surgery may be inferior. You accept our President's lie, do you not? These pirates and other leftists--Socialist-Democrats-- and hard-shelled liberals in the Congress--including the free-radicals called Tsarists--Olinsky-inspired bureaucrats wallowing in un-Constitutional power--working with the leftist administration, are going to destroy this great nation by their adamant, unforgiving, desperate, wicked will, by which phrase Churchhill described Hitler's Nazis. Already, Obama's backup will be cadres of

Highschoolers trained to condemn capitalism, border security, unfair industrializaion, and legal citizenship status in the US. To secure his next term in office, Obama is inviting illegals to cross our borders, who at a proper time will be declared legals unilaterally by Obama, himself--given Biodata cards like the rest of us--and ,mand made instant beneficiaries of Obamacare. They will constitute a 20- million voting block for his next term in office, if and when Amnesty arrives. You may absolutely count on that!! If you need open-heart surgery and can get it after 18 months, you may have to jump out of bed to mslr esu gpt sm an illegal vomplsininh og leg cramps while picking lettuce--if the Socialist-Democrat Federal Government will permit you to do so in order to express your genuine iternational sympathies for the Mexican indigent..

These and other political degenerates in the Congress --Amerika detestors and one-worlders--are determined to install Obmacare by the devious trickery of a reconciliation vote customarily for monetary bills) ,that will install the Senate version (as a rider) after the "deemed," the presumed, passage of the signed Senate version. And we, the people, do not see this ungrateful cheat on our will, our labor, our vision, our history? Tell me I successfully attended and graduated from Hollywod High, UCLA, Stanford U. I am an intelligent man. How can a bill not voted upon by the House...deemd to have passed... beome the law of the land, Constitutionally? It cannot. It is a paper law, a "law" in substance only, not in law. Unless, unless, a tyrant declares it to be a law without Constiltutional process. NOTE: -- Obama's raillery at "process." Now we see why he rebuks conservatives for their emphasis on "due process." He scorns the Constitution . The vote by the Senate on a major piece of legislation is a mere "process." Do you dumbed-down journalists get it? I'm sure you do and you find that Obama's end justifies the means of silence.

Without morals or ethics, these scavengers on democratic ideology will crow; At last we got Healthcare for all!"--ranslated meaning--State control of not one but all major industries in the US, the Marxist state, the debt 1.3 trillions of taxpayer dollars. And yet you are so stupid you do not see why people are out of work and have no consumer money to spend! You s...heads in power are a joke when it comes to brains; since even common sense carries a simple warning of catastrophy. Money? What is that to the leftists? Ours becomes theirs to spend without responsible contro, accountability or ethical conscience. Selah! We will get used to the tyranny, they say...like the frog in a pot of hot water that slowly heats up undetected by the frog that never jumps out before it is cooked.

Leaders? You would lead us down the "road to serfdom," you you empty-minded fatheads wthout a pot to render you in, your wisdom, and heartless chests swollen with illusury beneficince. You would make us servants to the government based on a failed European ideology that you somehow find acquaintance with and compatability with. I suspect it is convenient for your careers to do so. What colossal selfishness and the greed of Me-ism. You are delusional and drunk with power, all of you, the Prelates of Govement and the quibbling Scions of Journalism. That includes the President-- in your faces you followers of Rules for Radicals.instead of the US Constitution! No objections....

Where does it say: "The Congress shall represent a suitable ideology intead of the will of the people?

All new offices (Tsars) established by the Executive shall not represent the people, but rather delude the people in secret in order to promote the prosperity of all. Equality of virtue, talent, ambition and achievemen, though illusory, is the hailed product of tyranny. Making it so is the sword of power. Because you think Marxism will work in its coat of fashion called "Fascism" you, Mr. Presodemt. would impose on the American people, by guile, deceptiona and lies , instituted and led by Barack Obama, a regime alien to our history, repugnant to our people's will and destructive of our glorious history and the intentions of our Founding Fathers. Who do you think you are, since you speak from a radilcal, disconnecgted background. and not from the capacious space of risk, opportnity and rewards and liberty? Elected to be leaders, you hace become our tyrant overlord, regardless of our rejection of your alient and oppressive regime-plans. His Majesty Obama calls that "hope."

The Obamacare is in actualtiy a death-wish for America. It is an insult to our collective intellience as a people. It is a purgation of common sense and a ridicule of the God, whom Obama rarelyr mentions, He who who gave us our fundamental rights, not the State which you would create and have us to worship. America is wealthy because for over two hundred yrs we have invented, developed, invested in our ideas and projects and exploited our naturalr esources to bring this great nation to the position of exceptional wealth and visible production with God's help and our own initiative...these achievements in virtual isolationf from the rest ofthe world! You forget that America was an isolationist nation before Pearl Harbor awakened the giant. At this point in our history, we do not want Obama's fraudulent leadership. He sat in Wright's church for 20 years trying credibly to justify his distrustful hatred for America, He needed a pillory and he found it in Marxism. He is attempting to gtrtansform us into an image in economic and moral alignment with his mentor Saul and his ideology of Karl Marxs statism, the Socialist State. Olinsky"s Rules for Radials in your Chicago community. Those "Rules For Radicals"?

RULE # 1: The wealth of America has been accumulated at the expense of the rest of the world. If you gain a position of power apoligize to the billions of poor ripped off, exploited by American capitalists. Obama id strmping to efface the characgter of the American middle class, to e xpunge ilts enterprise and todestroy its vitality of initiative and enterprise...by depriving it of money! Edison, the Wright Brothers, Henry Ford linventedwithout money as Obama gauges its value.

But I tell you, Mister President, You never worked and sweated a day of your life at a skilled trade, day labor job, a business ownership. You're an elitist fraud who is above such common pursuits in life. When you promise to create more jobs, you don't know what you are talking about, Barack Hussein--America is wealthy not "at the expense of the rest of the world" but because of the above virtues of enterprise, inves\tment and hard work, as I say, in isolation largely unitl WW II. The rest of the world was so undevelopd that the alreadyimpoverished peoples had nothingwe could use or they could afford that ws made in the United States. We had all the coal, timber, factories, labor we needed. for ourselves. Rip offs...? Saudi oil is one exception. We shod them how to drill for oil..and now we are dependentuponthe Saudis. America as exploiter of the world? That;s the slosh from some brain-dead liberal Havard professor.

RULE #2 . Reverse the process by returning America's wealth to the poor and starving peoples of the rest of the world. (I have never heard mention of Appalachia!) Begin in America by massive taxation to make the exploiters the "greedy corporations" and private investors, i.e. Wall Street capitialists, know how it feels to be robbed of their wealth--your olossal Marxlist tyruth they will call a " lie.' Do so with dignity, statutory interpretations they will call "tricke/ Show a manner of " authenticity and calm. Let lies and bribery be two of your best tools. The ruck of the American people is too stupid to see through your schemes. That is your insight; they are deluded by a sense of their superiority before the rest of the world. They are a smug, presumptuous lot about their history. Ignore it. Ignore them. Learn to distance yourself.

RULE #3. Since Capitalist wealth was stolen by deception, deception is the name of the game you must play, behind locked doors when necessary. Do not listen to their appeals of simple-minded honesty. They are hypocrites; you are always--apology --almost always right.

RULE #4: Never admit that you are wrong, under any circumstances. That will only weaken your offense against monsterous capitalist greed. You must, however, be ruthless with the changes or enlightened socialism will not work. You are the bringer of new life to America. However,Disciple, you do not have the foggiest notion of what competiltion is.. All of your bailouts are free-throws from the foul line of unlawful encroachment called CEO firings and contractual re-arrangements. An anarchist, you are a law unto yourself, Worthy Disciple..

RULE #5: Mollify the discontents, for they lack the intelligence to discern your vision, or to appreciate all that can be done for them by the government. You can mollify them by small trade-offs, careful use of the word "jobs" to signify increases, and subtle expressions of sympathetic contenpt for the America AS IT IS... which has brought so much misery to the rest of the world. I will act with one swift blow...we will pass this bill by Easter (hallelujah, the risen Christ), a bill the American people are "entitled to." Utilize all other such expressions that conceal any cynicism and disdain for our capitalist, the so-called (controlled) democratic,free-market , entrepreneur system of government and ways of life. If this bill passes, the people will not, for a long time, have good faith and confidencer in their elected representatives, if they betray the people by voting YES for enllightened socialis leglislation. . Those who vote YES and live through the next decade will be filled with delight and saisfaction, but as Johnathan Edwards admonished the non-believers in his congregation one Sunday morning, "Too late! too late sinner ..beyond the reach of the love of God!"
Their religion is quiescent, placid, smug and accepting. You are an Activist: never for get that!

To the above names and all other leftists and hard-core liberals who push for bigger and bigger government through a medical agenda-- the heart of their so-called liberty--I tell you, their godless souls are not worth the cost of all the wars they have inspsired for money, Capitalist gailn and plunder. You abuse your power to realiize a defunct, speculative and corrupting ideology. You will make the selfishness of massive entitlements a virtue. You will, in doing so, feel that your are protected by the perfect justice of the"virtuous" socialist State.

Visit the fields of little white crosses above the cliffs at Normandy? Some drowned, some were shot, some lay in agony with wounds from mortars, mines, some were maimed, some survived to fight......but none ever, ever gave up fighting to the last because they were pawns of the Capitalists who s tayed home.. We must concel the European lifestyle of total dependence upon the government, Obama et al! Okay? Let the masses believe that they are the instrument of power and progress. Let those words be written in your face whenever you appear in public. Confidence!! Some of you Disciples may even findyour names on the WW II memorial in Washsington, DC.

I pray that God will bless any plan to rip America out of honst history by the roots in order to glorify your image as a Radical..   When it comes to warfare, homeland security and protection..and to economics and medicine for 300,000,000 people , most of you lifeless, spoiled-rotten freaks of elitist perpetuity don't know shit from Shinola. But you are are also weak at tilmes...aRadical ils a marked target for Capitalist expliters. . Maybe I should pray for you, because you will assuredly displease their God of creation, whom they deem to be the source sof source of wisdom for a city on a hill, one of a kind in human history,they believe, a threat to tyrants, a blessing to the suffering, a rock for the exile and a champion of justice.That is the dogma of theCapitalist, the propaganda o the American clon, the lies of a secretive nation of untold wealth stolen from the rest of the world.   Our strengths are not good enough for them, puky ounters of gold inthe marketplace, gold thieved rom the poor. . Your mindset is to trash traditions, Constituional powers when expedient, vitality of innovation, compassion in the charms of America. B careful of their charms; they are many. And let me caution you, my Dilsciples, that what I say in these Rules fof Radicals is , to my enlightened mind, incomprehensible to outsiders.

The Capitalists are the me-generation; they are a generation that lacks character. Go ahead. You've got to see to believe. The enemy is ready to hrow away 21st century America by their simple-minded, selfish concentration of power in Washington. The Capitalist Americans will never, ever gettheir free-wheeling grasping of money for their selfish use again, if you fllow my rules. zObama has determined to be famous in history regardless of the will of the people!

The Radical crap= sheet "Pravda of Chicago" printed these words at the start of Prfesildet Obama's term of office. "Bi-partisanahip, to you, Mister President, is achieved by the use of force to gain unity, and by force we here at the new"Pravda" mean:
1--seizure of whole industries, auto, banking, energy, media, education...
2--over-regulation that destroys competition, profit from competition is alien to the Govenment you envison, the marxist Stae.
3-- dishonest manipulation of statutory law, i.e First AmendmentRights
4--trash-disposal of Constitutional restraints,
5--corruption of the Congress with your money; you willhve lmany American as well as European supporters
6-- healthcare rationing, no death panel but shortages, shortages due to removal of ugly profit, This is a cleansing of the conscience.

7-- bribery of an entire state by the promise of free health care "forever

8--secret locked committee sessions,

9--a White House dinner to bribe the recalcitrant Senators and to fete our enemies with a forgiveness plate...free of charge!,

10--the use of financial reconciliation as a tactic to pass 9 pounds of confusing legislation, a bill of entangled enlightenment. They will learn the lessons of foesilght!

11--attempted control of the media by electronic incitements, pressure on media unions (supporters)

12--encouragement of political snitches!!

13-- lies (# 1: not everybody can get emergency medical care and or timely medical intervention. Your medical costs will go down.

14-- broken promises, broken promises are a part of the game! (Promise # 1: you can keep your own doctor. Tell them, Master.

15--necessary, spiraling taxation, its exact uses to be oncealed aailnsgt capitalist outcry. (See: sale of nationlal assets to raise funds for a bankrupt nation. The Chinese can manage Yosemite Park better than the Americans, anyway. This would e but another example of Communist freedom, no fee. to enter the park. The envious nations can hardly wait. I-10, becomes a cross-country toll road for Gemany's enrichment; The national parks bercome Spanish property. Bankrupt Amtrack becomes the property of a Japanese consortium. Tax-and- spendkeftusts in the Congress practice benevolent charity with a vengeance, Chicago's Pravda reprts. 16--delusional job-creation by the Federal government: When you tax to raise money to spend to "create" jobs, you destroy the base for the true creation by business because the government, by heavy taxes, remove their capacity to hire workers in the first place. It ils profit from which those workers are paid.

Vocal, democratic resistance is called "obstructionism." While you, President Obama, have silenced the mainstream media by the prostitution of their unions, and have enjoyed your jamboree with supportive public employee unions (includes UTLA) and have bought off fence-sitters in both Houses of Congress, you continue to plead a causus- belli against middle-class America. You're a case all right..of dishonest Chicago-barrio politics by means of a consortium of radical liberals and Lefists. The mobsters could not have done a better job of pay-off politics.

Pontius Pilate asked the crowd with derision, " What is truth?" with reference to "criminal" Christ's teachings. Truth to Pilate was the sword. The Truth to you, Mister President, is the sword of Federal power used to abuse the people--by intimidation, like a bully, and fiscal exhaustion--driving a free people into compliance with a foreign doctrine and theory of governmen that has never worked, ever, ever. Instead of blood, the surrender of our freedoms to taxation and Federal control of our entire lives will cause to perish the gleaming battlement and holy offerings of suffrance we are able, thus far, to extend to the rest of the world. Where inWestern History has the United States ever approached the rest of the world to beg, to capture, to enslave, toexploit and rapaciously, to impoverish?

Your sword of abuse of Federal power will extinguish the light of liberty forever in this great nation. Not we or our children, or their children for genrations to come will ever forgive you misguided, nepotistic,, sychophabntic, blood suckers, thieves because you would cut out the heart of this nation. The words of those who love this country will not go unanswered or ignored by future generaions when they see how we stood in the breech to fight you parasites on liberty. Can you say you love your wife if you send her out onto street to whore for you...because a putah named Ansky prescribes the action for an ideology, the ideology of tyrants, as total submission to the State

THE CRISISs, b y Charles E. Miller

POSTSCRIPT: There is much that can e said, by way of example s in hou history, to the matter of submission to te State. America was fouded on therejection of that idea, that a peoplew ho understood freedom should submit to the oppressive mandates, taxes and regulatins of a kingand a Parliament whose existence bor eheavily upothem b ut who had no voice in the actions of the monarch or his henchmen inthe House of Lord Istead, we are today faced with the prospect f subissinto anevery-growing overnment,fromthe kind oflihtbulsbs we mustuse to the kinds of cars we ut drive. the American spirsit will g onlyso far; the enemhy underestim;ates the tenacity and resiliance of the people. Theywill learn, not onlyh in the 2012 election but imn the people's refusal tob e so micro-managed they cannot enjoy a tea party without the state olice itruding upontheir fee association. The government will attempt to manage the 2nd Amendment to the Constitution, but they will not succeed. This is not Hitler's Germany whose people knew only the tyrants of small Duchies, the amalgamation of power by emperors and barons and the silencing of the serf voice of freedom by paid soldiers sof the Medieval rulers. We are not accustomed to that sort of tyranny in America, and we will eventually rebe as our Declaratinof Indepedence admonishes us to do-- "...that whenever any form of governmetn becomes destructive of these ends (right to life, liberty and the pursuit of happiiness) it is the Right of the people to alter or abolish it." It makes me happy to read by an incadescent light, the red rays emitted being harmless to my eyes. therefore, I shall pursue that simple happiess, and stuff it the Federal government. Period. If I owned an acre of land the government called "wet-land" that had not seen water except for rain in decades. Iw ould buyild upon it, and to the privy with the federal government. Let them pull down my house, charg\e me and I would not pay. Go to prison, perhaps...It was my happiness ot build upon the land that God gave me. Clear? We, the Americans, a re not your serfs , your toadies, your go-for's.

TO HELL WITH MADISON'S CONSTITUTION IF IT OBSTRUCTS GLORIOUS MARX

`Citizen.

Amendments 13, 14 and 15 are commonl\y referred to as the "Civil War Amendments," Their provisions and obligations applied to the States during the Reconsruction Period after the Civil War. By their context, is was aobbous that they were to include the Rebel States upon completio of their term of probaton after the war.

Sen.Chuck Schumer (D) of NewYork has encouraged Barack Obama to skirt the authority of the Congress by personally, as President, unlulaterally raising the "debt ceiling" by contracing for a loan from a ceeditor nation, ,doubtless, Red China.

Curious as to what provision in Amendmen XIV Obama was to use for this criminal violation of Executive power, I found the passage of deceptive misuse in Section 4 of that Amendment:

The words refer to the debt incurred in the War by the States, both North and South, the readmission of a defecting State bearing the obligation to conform. "THE VALIDITY OF THE PULIC DEBT OF THE UNITED STATES AUTHORIZED BY LAW, INCLUDING DEBTS INCURRED FOR PAYMENT OF PENSIONS AND BOUNTIES FOR SERVICES IN SUPPRESSING INSURRECTIONS OR REBELLIONS SHALL NOT BE QUESTIONED."

NOTE: The XIVth Amendment gives VALIDITY to the debt legitimately incurred in the Civil War. It does not authorize an INCREASE in the national debt incurred 146 years later either by a Presidental Executive Order or a unilateral action to obligate the United States to a higher National debt limit, in transgression and criminal vioation of Article I, Section 8 of the US Constittution. "The Congress shall have the power...to brrow money on the credit of the United States." Becuse the people are the debtyors by way of taxation, our Founders wisely reposed that power to borrow in the hands of lhe Congress, the lower House to initiate the loan...not the President.

The Schumer-Obma enablement would lift the passage out of context.   Section 4 of the Amendment continues: "But neither the United States nor any State shall assume or pay any debt or obligation incurred in aid of insurrection or rebellion against the United Sates or any claim for the loss or emancipation of an slave; but all such debts, obligations and claims shall be held illegal and void." Thefe ils h ;command or specificliy. The Schumer-Obama arrangemen conveniently omits any ;and all details of usage itemization. Why? Rememering that Obama is a Marxist, we can knowilngly assume gthat the distrilbution of America's wealh , its destinations, usage and recipients are all lirrelevant details to the main purpose of spreading the wealth. The Admilnistration will secretlydecide who "needs" the money!

In other words, the slaves were free; owners could not charge the people for their loss. This provision was irrelevant to the Schumer-Obama conspiracy," if one may call it that. Obama would use just that part of the XIVth Amendment thatg IL have placed in caps.

Such an egregious violation both of the President's oath of office and of the Constiution's express lmnits on the Exeutive Branch is an impeachable offense on two grounds
(1) It violates the fundamental Separation of Powers made evident by the structure and the content and intentions of the Founders, to limit the powers of each of the three branches; and to deny the power to any one branch to usurp the powers of another Branch, or to exceed the limits so stated in the the words and clar injunctions and provisions Constitution. Today we have active legislating from the Bench by the Supreme Court and the liberal lower courts. We have the formtion of new bureaus that are a law unto themselves, wthout Congressional oversight, as the 40 Czars.

(2) Such an abuse of Executive power is not granted to the President, nor is it implied in the limits placed upon the Congress to admit, require, consider or sanction the Executive's over-reaching abuse of his Article II powers. Sen. Schumer cannot, therefore, speak for the entire Senate, nor, indeeed, for the House of Representatives which has the Consitutional , sole authorty to collect moneies for the Federal Government.

Clearly, the President's seeking a loan. He would thereby unilaterally raise the debt limit. His act would would be a usurpation of the authority of the House or Representatives, as set forth in Article I , Section 8 "The Congerss shall have tle Power to lay, and collect Taxes, Duties, Imposts and Excises...." Such a unilateral move would violate his oath of office, "to protect and defend the Constitution of the United States...." The President does not have that power. Any perversion of the XIVth Amendmen to accomplish that purpose would be grounds for Presidient Obama's impeachment.

It's time we got rid of tlese outlaws in our government, That Schumer and Obama should even consider such a crminal offense is a reflection of Obama's devous character, his fundamenal dishonesy and his ideological intentions to destroy historical America wile he is in office.

THE CRISIS, by Charles E. :Miller 7-7-11 .

POSTSCIPT: So that any reader of the above argumnet will not be deceved, I am a poet, not a lawyer ,havIng taken Ihe 1st year of law school. However, I undrstand contracts.

of which the President's oath of office is an example of a supreme contract. The Presidents injudicious and dishonst conideration of the unlawful a vilabillity of the AmendmenIXIV sepsaks to the Amerilcanjury of taxpayng citizens of their right of protest andtheir protection, basically and irreversably, of the Law ofthe Land. If the President ofthe United Sttes boligaes hmself to the cult ofdishonesty in t he manner IL have described, what isto be done? As LI hv escrilvbed, the usurption contilns no l details as to the distribution of our wealth...to whom, his Chicago cronies, the Alinsky's inthe Administration, tothe supposedly poor who f awn upon his every move, yea, even to the propagandist Media who kiss his hand like the Pope's and remain silent about his buses of power. Therefore, itwill be had to block that distribution of our monies, our initiative and our hnor. The taxpayers would be regarded bythe liberal press as highwaymen intentuponstopping the stage of so noble a rival for christendom. The s hort answer is simply to throw the brigands out of power with the 1112 election and allow the simpering, cowardly sribblers in the Liberal media to rot on the vines of American luxury. It does not take a wise or an intelligent man to break the law. Any fool can do it, and he has and will continue to do so until we clean house.

KING GEORGE COPY-CAT

Citizen.

The President who compares his sleezy spendthrift program for the last nine months with the cause for and character of our history is a charlatan, a liar to the world, an appeaser to their envy and to the honor of our enemies, and a blind guide to the naive and unlearned. Is his performance the equal in character and inrtelligence to our pioneer hisory, to our wars to free the peoples of the world, our compassion after in calamities worldwide, to our hardy growth from New England colonies, through the Cumberland Gap westward to the Pacific ocean,to our mighty developments in industry at the turn of the 19th centujry and tothe inspiration of our founding documents to the present excdptionalism and our recognition that an omnipoten tGod--not the government-- is the source and guaranto of our life, liberty and the pursuit of happiness.Barack Obm' puny Mxi ;;mins does not grasp these realities of our real trandformation. He seeks, insgtead, to expunge from our memories of he past their historical acualities and supplant that history with the ideology of a Briltilsh madman named Marx. That is delusory by any ;measure, more than a fixation, a convicion t hat hecan accomplish in fourtoellight years the total obliteration of that great historical past and in its place put the fraudulent promise of a depraved, suject and slave pople and their third-world economy. lObama would kyte his philosophy, his third-world vision over afree nation of 300 million individuals living in the confidence that theirs is a free nation. His sole premise, the Marxian dogma of "spreadilng thewealth," ils t hat our brilliance as a ation was gotten illegaly, illegitimately, that we are parasilted upn the rest of tlhe world. His simplistic thinking is not just theresult f Harvard andEast chicago brailnwashing; it is theresult of a sick delusion of subsgtitutionary power, achieved chiefly by ipoverishsing the American people andmaking themdependentupon the Federal Government. That vision, that hope bythe charlatan in the White House, is not just draconian and unrealistic; it is sick.

Instead, let me cite from the Declaration of Independence the transgressions upon our history by the Obama program, become visible these last nine months. He proclaimed at his recent UN Speech that he was the "king of kings," usurping Christ's place in the context of Holy Scripture.

Let us state the rulings (we know not all his Executive Orders) that dismay a noble and great people.

1) "He has erected a multitude of offices, and sent/appointed Swarms of Officers to harrass our People and eat out their Substance.(expansion of present DC agencies and surrounding Officers of His Administration that includes Tsars and every conceivable mode for the exercise of political power by his adminstration. He has failed consistently to submit his Executive Orders to the Congress for their approval, but, instead, has ordered that they be executed wthout pause or query. The silent media have been complicit in this mode of

Presidential secrecy, a fact that augers ill for this nation of free individuals. . A tyrant who acts in secret and without the consent of the body that represents the will of the people acts corruptly, both out of the will of God and out of the law of the land. The Health Care, the Cap andTax are but starters, for he has passed the one with duplicitous maneuvering between the Houses, and it can be expected that he will coerce into law the latter in the same manner, deceitfully without a hand-count.

He has kept among us in times of peace, standing Army withoutt he Conent of our Legislatures. (FEMA, the EPA,IRS, Czars) They can take away the use of our land, close up our shops, declarewhat is sprivate to be public, grant token amensty to hordes of invaders as the King's men, brokenfaih with their oath of office and treated the commom people, linheritors f our nation's brilliant history a s cheap dung who merilt the oss of their exceptional country and subjection, political ans social, that compareswith the sufering mankind of third-world coutries. Preslident Obama is an Amerilcan lin name only; he a heathen iposter who is not averse t grandeloquent dilsplays sof persoal power and mischievous aneuverings of power to achievehis third-world vision for America. He has proposed, initiallyby suggestion only, an INS, National security force "as well trained and as well funded as the military." This can be taken to mean a national police force, as in Fascist, Nazi Europe which will be, or can be, activated by meana of the Biodata card that all citizens will be ordered to carry. .

3) He has affected (coming) to render the Military independent and superior to the Citizen Power. (His National Service forces to come)

4) He has combined with others to subject us to a jurilsdition foreign to our Constitution and unacknowledged by our Laws, giving his Assent to their Acts of pretended Legislation. (Appeals hy justices, his appointees, to our Supreme Court that accept or imitate foreign rulings by the Hague Court of three judges in Amsterdam) H hasencouraged an openness to Sharia law==whee practilcl-- proclaimed pubically by liberal SC judges open to Sharia law President Obama has encouraged legislation from the bench by the silmple expedient of acknowledging the expedience of his appointees--not their knowledge and application of Constitutional law--this possition by liberal justices, his appointees, being conducted without Congress's approval. He has refused to endorse the enactment of tort reform e.g. the Obamacare bill, , since his final official support in large measure comes from trial lawyer who will fleezethe people for vciolations based on a bill never read by either House before ilts passage...a mysery ill ine very sense of the word. . We willunderstand what is inthe bill when the time comes, sailth Mme Pelosi. .

5) For imposing taxes on us without our Consent. He has raised our natioal debt to at east 14 trillions dollars yet has not given usan inkling as to how he will use the borrowed money. That isthe work of a cheat and athief, a posseur and a scapgrace eore the eyes of the people.

6)....For altering fundamentally the Forms of our govenment.

Siince he took office, our President, elected by the free will and choice of the people, he has designed a program that advances not the values of free men, values of honesty in government and probity in public conduct, but he has, instead, concealing his true intentions, driven this nation's debt further into the darkness of total destruction, the economy of a bankrupt people who know not the limits to their capacity to govern with moral discretion and judicious honesty. .The people are in rebellion; let the liberal Democrats, in particular, in the Congress beware--they call us "terrorists"-- for as the conservative govement grows, so will the atttude and power of the people turn out the offenders from the seats of power. We remain a free people only insofar as we act to unseat the present demi-gods of power and founders of our astonishing debt produced by greed and the unattentive trust in a great people. We know that our President campaigned under false colors...as a loyal American though acually an anti-American Marxist. He detests profit, not realzing that it is the excess from consummer purchases that is used to grow jobs, not pathetically produce depdence by debt and entitlements, as does a Government bailout that grows dependency.   He is loyal, by his own action, to the foreign agenda, the alien ideology of the Marxist state, which is but a short distance from the damnations of political tyranny. He can hae no plan xcept tht of Marx! So don't expect a plan or a budget from him. His only plan is to subvert a people.   Barack Obama is a subversie in every sense of the meaning of that word. He is subverting the people's will, their customs, history and their intelligence. His only real power is the power of the purse. I think now that he sees that.

THE CRISIS, by Charles E :Miller

POSTSCIPT: Our Founding Fathers realized that we could ot be at one and the same time a free people yet be governed by a king thousands sof miles distant. There hlad obe a cleanbreak wih Briltish power and the rulimng Parliament. This move requirederaordinary courage and foresight; for the Founders had to devise a document, after d=eclarinf the independence, tlhat woudl stand thetests of time, malefacgors like our present President,whofor one reasonr another, always crrupt, desir eto transform America into another v ision,that of the Old World. ILt took eight ylears of bloody war agailnst lincalculable odds to beat the well trailned andwell equipped Briltish army. We had one advantage, nay, two advantags. (s) We were rilghing on our own soil and we had a courage and a dynamic will for reeedom the Briltlishdid not comprehend. We lhad thecpacity, therefore, to fight against great odds, and that we did. The slingular characerilstic of the past two and a halfl years sof Obamas regime is its blidnness to thatose factorslin our history. ILgnoring the will ofthe people theregime li washington has also ilgnored our history and the sources of tis strength, lindependence, mutcourage, faith inthe scope, context, genesis and purposes of our nation.   We willovercome thesubversives preenly in washngton DC. They lack thestrenth, linner ortllitude, that downthrough human histor has enabled civilized men to overcomethe barbarians presently in power. In real sense of the word, the present sychophantic, opprssive, ieological administratin is barbaric. They look an speak the same as we out here in greater America; but we are not the same...whatsoever/ They are the barbarlians who woould   reduce us to man-worship...as p;unishmn for sour leechery and parasitical offenses again the rest of the wrorld. That is the classic first-lie of Obama;s administration, a power-hungrykind of the ignorant maurauders., Ameicans. Such is the maniacal egomania of our present messianic Presildent.

TRANSFORM AMERICA

Citizen.

The Obamacare bill "passed" by the House and announced by Neo-Marxist Pelosi as 220 to 211 is a fraudsulent piece of legislaion for two reasons:

    1) It is a bill intended as a tax bill chiefly to raise revenue for the benefit of poiticians and trial lawyers. There is very little medical relief contained in the bill, certainly less than is now obstainable under our present system of health care. The bill should therefore have originated in the House of Representatives, according to Article I, Section 7 of the US Constitution. "All Bills for raising Revenue shall originate in the House of Representatives...." A tax bill was dlisguised as a"care" bill.

    2) The bill did not come as an exact text from the Senate, which is the scope and content and manner of lawful transmission from one House to th other House. Art I, Sec 7: "Every Bill which whall hve passed the House of Representaive and the Senate...." Another bill, bill(s) ? One text only . It came, instead, as a presumed, a "deemed passed" piece of legislation. The House did not vote on the actual Senate Text. They voted on the Reconciliation bill, a composition of "fixes": to the Senate text. Therefore, the manner and textual configuration of the transmission was unlawful and in violation of Article I, Section 7 of the Constitution. 1. The House did not vote on the Senate bill; they voted on the "f ixes." The President signed a bill that was never voted upon by the House of Representatives. It is therefore raudulent as valid legislation and subject to violations and/or repeal.

    Thus, even though House rules admit that a bill whick is "deemed" to have passed, a Byrd rule for Budget recnciliations only, represents a Senate bill that has been presumably voted upon but has not actually been voted upon, that legilsltion represents a fraudulent concurrence of both houses. The House cannot deem to have passed a major legislation without a House vote. Article I, Section 7. That deceptive interpretation put upon transmissiona and passaage of a major 2,000 page plus bill is subject to challenge in the courts. Strict interprtation of Section 7, Article I of the Constitution requires that a bill moving from one House to the other requires a vote, not the assumption of a vote. A vote by either House must show majority concurrence and agreement by name-calling vote In this case, passage was by the mandate of an assumed i.e "deemed" vote by the House.

The bill was conceived and composed fo the benefil of politicians and trial lawyers, Obama supporters and it, Its fraudulent manner of passage therefore betrays its illeglitimacy of ovrweening power conrol by a one-pary Congress. The hasty and chalatan manner of passage also reveals....

(a) Obama's antipathy towardt he voting people of this Republic, and
(b) a bribery of his supporters to pass the bill regardless of the will of the people. by imputing to them ignorance and stupidity demonstragtes his tyranny in the matter.
(c) The people, by their vote express their assent or dissent from legislation. Thus, by the omission of the representative vote by the House, the bill stands as unlawful and Constitutionally irrelevant to the will of the people. Its mandate that the uninsured purchase insurance ils u;nconstitutional. 'That porocess has already started, hundeds of waivers hving already been granted. The people through the deceptions. Pelosi's perverse interpretation of "passed" to mean" voted upon" by the House violates the letter and the spirit of the Constitution.

Our Founders did not devise, compose and pass the Constitution for the benefit of politicians, trial lawers, bureaucrats or any and all appointees of the Federal Government. It passed our Constituion in 1789 in a language all literate persons can understand. It is a law by. with and for the people. It was not intended to adorn the reputation of a self-seeking Kensyan politician.

Therefore, any literate citizen has the legal, Constitutional and historical standing to oppose Obamacare. This is our country, not Washinton's If violence should come as an offshoot, a reaction to , a passionate opposition by Amerians to Obamacare, it will not be civil or a piecemeal thing but will represent a people who rise up to put corrupt poliicians out of power and ltlhereby to recognie the lgitimate powers of the Federal government under our Constitution. For it is power they seek, not leadership. By the seizure of unlasul power over our lives, they show contempt for America, these socialist-democrats. Like Obama, they wish to " completely TRANSFORM the country.

If I changed into a grizzly bear, there will nothing left to remind others that I was once a man. That is his vision for Amerca. HIS WORDS . to " completely transform" America. There, by this logic, Barack Obama, Pelosi, Reid and the other complicit pirates are anti-Americans, throw in frothing meatball Chris Matthws and idiot Paperwad Keith Oberman as well. TRANSFORMATION IS A WORD THAT SIGNIFIES TOTALITY OF CHANGE, anything less than that transformation is alteration, modification, simply change or rennovation.

Remember, with regards to the violent opposiion, that in 1775 we had an entire British army who had invaded our shores. Now,we have a civil opposition which, in the interests of keeping the fabric of this nation sound, whole and lawful, men of wisdom and discenment recommend against violence.

Also, do not forget that the bill is fraudulents for the above reasons; at best it is bad law and should be so considered. It can be repealed state by state, under Amendment 10 of the Bill of rights, powers reserved to the States if not by enumeration given to the Government. AMENDMENT 10--"The powers not delegated to theUnited States by the Constitution, nor prohibited by it to the States, are reserved to the State srespectively, or to the people." Those powers are no reserved to the socialist pirates in the Congrss and in the administration.

The Founders wrote the US Constitution chiefly toprotect the people from big government, from tyrants, from a king, a dictator, a Marxist/ TheConsiltution was writtenilnthelanguage of the people. The Founders westld wlith ideas to compose a docu;ment assessible to the people's reading, their understanding, their applicaion and their acceptance. Washington, DC has primary authority over governance? Their authority is seondary to that of the American people. This is our country. The politicians serve us,not the other way aroound. We do not serve you or your appointees or your radical destroyers nor, when we learn better, your radical agenda for us. .

AUTOMATONIC AMERICA...BROKEN PROMISES

You can keep your own insurance policy
You can keep your own doctors--;
"Let me be clear--
Insurers will be brought to heel
You will get tax credit for your policy
Small businesses will get get a tax credut for insurering their employees
Shovel-ready Jobs will be created by the governmet
Those families with two or three children will receive tax credits
There will be transparency in my administration
I will totallyeliminate ear marks
Insurerers can no longer raise skyrocket rates
Insurers can no longer reject pre-existing conditions,ulcers, paralysis, cancer
There will be fostered competetion bewen insurers that ill reduce rates;
government will enter the competition
Government will not cause the disappearance of favored linsurerers
Integrity will be our motto: no deception in government Five hundrfed thousand
new jobs (federal)
Every child a college education
Green energy will replace fossil fuels
Other nations will respect my diplomatic outreach in their lust for power
Security and safety of the people through discussion with our enemies. They
canno be shooting while they are talking. (Pearl Harbor,what's that?
The ends justify the means

Fraud, incompetnce,waste and human error abound. If you suppose that 300 millions citizens can function one year or twenty years down the road like a machine under the above fiats of Obamacare and oppressive reulations, you are literally stupid or irretrievably naive or mad in your denial of reality. Socialist Obama must absolutely reduce us to an abject third-world country if he even expects us to function accordingto the above provisions of Obamcare and other agenca policies. Remember, to "transform" as Obama promises signifies TOTALITY OF CHANGE. as from man into a grizzly, a nation into fifedoms of socio-economic classes, a free people into obedient and intimidated serfs, a government into a tyranny, a free-trade economy into a totally regulated distribution of Centrally prescribed goods that will be rationed out according to pre-determined" needs." Stricken as eventful and consequenial in social life willbe the God-given conscience; the state will be your conscience. The intimidaion will include confiscation of your property, considering it to be a luxury unfair to those without. Things will seem to be normal, like voting--one party, one candidate. Opporunity for the people will transform into opportunism for the politicians and their sychopnhants. Human rights will b a sham, a dim mentory of our siatsant and unbelievable (bralnwashed) Declaration of Independence.

Consider the present intrusion of Washington into our lives:
Car indusgtry--Federal ownership; design regulations
Banking Industey--loan-money control
Mortgage Industry--regulations
Investment Industry--regulations
Insurance Industry--competition with Govt.
Education by DOE and viz a viz one source loans , TV propagandizing kids in the grades by Obama' illegal inclusion; tuiton control
Defense Industry--dangeeous reduction
Housing Industry= including hotels--bankrupcy, homelesness
Healthcare Indusry-destrucion
Media industry-capured Agitprop
Transportation Industry--
Communication Industry--propagada
Pharmaceutical Industry--removalof critical drugs
Diary/Farming/Ranching Industries (EPA conrols on land, water usage) land control, methane oversilht
Food Indusr--packing, canning, etc.--regulations
Retail Stores Industry. incl. restaurants--uncerainty, regulations,closures
Elecronics Industry--China's conrol
Entertainment Indusry--content control
Libraries--closures
Volunteer Organizations (non-profit) Red Cross
Remaining: religion and the internet

Staggers the imagintion: these Industries and organizations represent the achievements of a free Americian people who enjoy the fruits of liberty, opportunity and individualism are now captive to the Federal overnment! These achievements have enabled us to rescue the rest of the world. Remember: the Feeral Goernmen created none of these. . Small men who lack enterprise. imagination and love for America would--for personal power and control of the people--exploit the power accorded their offices by the Constitution.
   The above industries are the creations of the people for the people who by diligence, inventivemess. initiative, competition , native and learned skills and hard work under liberty brought about these industries! Thus has the God of our forebearers blessed us.

But the tyrannical seizure of these enterprises is an act of piracy by the Federal Government and is anti-American in nature, intent and spirit. Because these industries no longer belong to the people, they have been STOLEN from the people and used against them to put them into a mode of abject enslavement to the State. At last we have "caught up with the rest of the world!" What a contemptible lie , Madam Pelosi!

There comes a breaking point at which arms may be necessary to repel the power-hungry pirates who swarm down upon us from Washinton, DC. The Gestapo thugs doing the bidding of Obama will be the IRS, who are without guns but will use our lawws against us to subdue us. The knock' won't be at midnight but in the bright sunlight but that knock will be twice as dangerous to your happiness because instead of disappearing into a slave camp you will be interred into a prision of trillion-dollar indebtedness or fined , the penalty pending, since the IRS will now have access to your bank account, and to your portfolio to ferret out cheats in a growing atmosphere of suspicion, as always goes with a tyrannical state. We stand on the precipice of these TRANSFORMATIONS happening. Remember Obama's promise. I intend " to completely transform America."

Think about these things, you 40% who see Obama as a reasonable facsimile of the risen Christ for this nation.

THE CRISIS, by Charles E. Miller 4-9-10

POSTSCRIPT: No other administration in American history hasd emonstated such a degree, extent and manner of power control as the present Obama Administration That control is the work of outlaws, from Obama to the Czas, from the liberals and leftsts ingovernment to the lackeys in the media. Their willingness to scrap the US Const\ttion is the work of outlaws who believe they know better than our Founders and the informed American people. Rebelling, by committingact of un-Constiltutional Naural man's outlawry, of rebellion agaist founded authority will work its will against us, the people. In all of its political sophisticaions, that outlawy is symptmatic of man's capacity to rebel as an act of his sin nature. ht ils anarchy, ;not freedom, for feedom infers a base of obedience to law. Originally in the Garden, it was God's law. Man is not naturally good, corrupted by society. He is a naturally wicked, evil creature who finds means, mechanisms, instruments by which he can give voice and action to that rebelllious nature, in his pride dismissing his evil work as necessary f or the good of mankind and for the establishment of fairness. His rebellious sin-nature makes of hman a inicpient outlaw. Laws control that basic natural man In a society intended to promote peace and prosperity, the law is warped, perverted, distorted to accord with the dark side of his nature. The Natural Man will attempt to conceal his sin nature by manufacured disguises, whether by laws that favor his utopian vision, or by constraints that modify his rebellion opponents. But the natural man cannot be eradicated, even by a relilgious faith. More often than not the work of governmental outlaws must be mollified by laws that subdue free men in order to form, not a more perfect union, but a tyrannical state of obedient sefrs. We are headed in that direction under Obma and his ilk in Washington DC. Civilized men will have to vote him and his deux ex macina out of power.

DEBT LANGUAGE OF DECEPTION

Citizen

We understand the cry belittling the slow and pessimistic growth of the economy from our "tired old politics of the past" republicanism. Yet we have been around much longer, most of us, than you and we have tried your means of economic growth via heavy-handed taxation. We have found that the money that would enable entrepreneurs to hire more workers, improve a product or a service, enlarge their consumer base though advertising and customer satisfaction goes into Oba,a's pocket (e.g unions, special-nterests supporters) and into the pockets of the Socialists who now control the government (increased agency employments, expansion of regulations, Chicago gangster style extortionists) . You, President Obama, , are a colossal failure with your agenda of tax and spend. You and your lickspittle pirates in Washington, the Congress and the Adminisration, don't really know what the hell you are doing and could not care less except that the money that the people work for puts you, keeps you, in office. A plague on the lot of you,...sir. Your Statism will ultimatelydestroy the source of your profligate spending wealth. That is a promise based onthe hstorical outreac of Marxist socialism, Obama;s ploy, his policy inspiration, his efaul llin leadership as President.

We are neither stupid nor inexperienced in such matters, much to Obama's surrmise and denegration. But we know whereof we speak. You "big shot," were a pukey kid when we were growing businesses, and profit. You presume that you know more, an arrogant presumption informed by your ignorance and suppositious gang of select cronies who cling to you like their gamgster godfather. Our experience is --that you cannot grow the eonomy by using our tax money (and borrowing unconscionably from an enemy nation, Red China) as you continue to spend spend without conscience or plan and thereby to add more agencies and personnel to the Federal employee rolls and entitlements to the "deserving.Because you have no work ethic, that growth is illusory to y ou. Our esperience is -- that as you attempt to exert more and more authoriy over our everyday lives in order to succor your vanity and pride and to armor the administration with bureaucrats, that you are fast becoming the enemy of the people. YWe understand work, competitionand achievement. You understand only lust,seizure, control. The first requires individual energy and effort; the latter demands controland power.

You, sir, Miser Obama, are an incompetent. I don't say that lightly Apparently thinking yourself to be led of God, as did Hitler in the 1930's to draw the Luthern church into his orbit, you are in the process of destroying a beautiful, vibrant, productiv, optimistic America and converting her into a European third-world nation. There is only one way to stop this process of intimidationa, destructiona and erosion of our liberties and that is to get rid of you and your gang of pirates on the Hill. And we shall. Like your mentors Marx and Olinsky, you have underestimated the middle class. We do not have a history of peonage and servile submission to Feudal control by a baronial government. You lie about our history, ignoramus; you lie about our achievemens, insulter; you lie about our gifts of blood and treasure to the world, hell's deceiver; you lie about our prosperity, blind man; you lie about our needs and our capacities for growth, supid aggrandizer; you lie bout our past mistakes, unforgiving interloper. Lie upon lie. Alinksy's " Rules For Radcals" encourages his followers to lie, since the Americans are not worth honest confrontation or moral approval. Lying to our faces is your second nature, Barack Hussein Obama. Lying to the people is a plague among the Washington elites in the Congress, administration...and an example to your fawning, insufferable, non-entity surrogates, the liberal media. Smile

But our money will go only so far, despite your golden rhetoric. So we who have more proven common sense than either you or your administration put together, are slow to accept and, indeed, even to listen to your tired old third-world rhetoric of the Government's spending our way into prosperity by the expediency of hiring more workers with taxpayer money the which foolish squandering of the people's money provided you with the arrogance to boast of job creation. You are a deceitful man with a anti-American education and that makes you dangerous to our future. You verbalize every crisis and exigency of government by sweet talk and that makes you treacherous to our future as a nation. Your clapperclaw administration brates about job growth and economic recovery. But those triumphs, sir, are an illusion you cannot project upomn us, for we know better. They conform to the old saying of robbling Peter to pay Paul. The money simply changes hands from the hands of the earners into the hands of the spenders in DC. as the governement grows. Wealth grows by the exchange of money from consumers into the hands of entrepreneurs enabling them to hire, to improve a produce or service and to draw new comsumers. Your dull , branwashed intellect does not comprehend the formula for economic i.e capitalist growh because the very word means damnation in your mind. Organization without growth is pointless, Mr. Community Organizer. We are not fooled in the least.

Those alleged new jobs are simply Federal jobs, temporary, non-wealth-creating jobs. They shrink,they do not grow the general economy Those new hirees are not private-sector employees, they are federal employees and it is not the economy that grows, sir, it the government that grows. Who do you think you are fooling?

You are going to lose in the next election because you have taken the American people to be fools, have picked their pockets, have invaded their lives like federal worms of gnawing control, and have jeopardized the entire future of this country by trillions of debt that will bankrupt America when our et, as it will, surpassed our GNP. .Greece all over. You will keep it up because you distrust and detest this great nation and wish to reduce us to beggary in the eyes of the world yet call it growth, thinking we are deceived. Smile,Scratch.

Plain as it may be, logically, real private-sector growth is not acceptable to you because of your socialist fixation on power to manage. It is not the Federal power to manage that distributes the wealth and that upscales the economy. It is the private experience and freedom to invest money (providng the Government does not take all the ilnvestment capital) that creates business, industry, employment the which upscale the economy. Entrepreneurs, not the elitist penthousers of Washington, are the source of America's prosperty. We are and have been from the start a mechantile nation, not an agrarian country with a feudal history. You are oily-tongued but also an ignoramus about our history, and that is another dangerous combination. Slick Sheister.

You and your administration would, I believe, feel more at home operating out of Berlin or Paris or Anthwerp or Moscow. None of these courtries has a large middle-class. None is a merchantile nation. We are excptional. You share with them the Medieval baronial heritage of power control over the worker serfs below the castle, the White House castle. You and your socialist philosophy are retrogressive in the scale of civilization'sprogress to impove mankind's lot. You actually are convinced, being an idealogue, that you do us a favor with Obamacare. You and the Congress will screw up our world's finest system of healthcare, permanenly. The plan is so complex and the governmen so inept and you, sir, and your lynchpin surrogates so incapable that we will retogress into some sort of abyss of medical and communication mistakess, shortages in medicines , doctors, nurses, drugs and devices, inadequacies in hospital beds--back to time warp of the middle ages in healthcare,,,and linerest once again in the Four Humours. Then will come your damned comparisons with socialist progress in Europe, you European dog with fleas that have to be scratched.

A disease will be cured by bleeding with leeches, the bureaucrats. a broken leg will be splinted with a tree limb while the patient waits in a long line. An attendee may have to set the leg due to a shortage of orthopaedic doctors. . Pacemakers will become a thing of science fiction. Your godless tangle of mischievous ordinances and references will totally destroy trust, efficiency and achievement in the medical field. But you Trotskyites are blinded by your ideology and cannot forsee that. That is a promise. That shortage of doctors will give rise to quackery, dangerous operations, home remedies, exotic herbology, open arket on drugs, shortages in medicines and no more wonder drugs...and suicides...dark-ages stuff. We, the American people, will do our damnedest to rescind your pot-luck medicine, Obama. In any event, Obamacare is a fraudulent and un-Constitutional bill because it did not receive a vote by the House of Representatives. "Deeming" passage is not a vote, it is an assumption only. Obmacare is mere trickery of a corrupt House. The contents of the bill are a tangle of error, inadequacies and shortages. Do you acually think you can effectively and competently treat the health care of over 300 million people? Appaently you do, or want us to bellive that you do. You, sir, are a damned fool as are those Trotskyites who side with you, Pelosi, Reid et al ! You are a Mammon-ite and an American-ite.

Actually, like your mentors Alinsky and Marx, you do not understand the American middle-class because you did not grow up in the middle class. That is one source of your ignorance. I live in a neighborhood of old crumbling, run down shacks worth a quarter of a million, whilst you, sir, live in on your White penthouse on Capitol Hill, paid for by the best "workers of the world, unite"-ed, the American people. You and your Socialist ilk are unreal. We are united behind and in our system of government and our ways of life, unique and exceptional before the world, govened by a Constitution and involed in ways which you disdain and corrupt. You, sir, are all screwed up about America's economy. Your deliberately dishonest performance in 18 months, based on that Ideologue illusion of a Socialist government that is virtuous. Your delusory state of mind makes you treacherous to our nation's future. You, sir are not the well-spring of our Founders' faith. You are the sinkhole of distrust of the people and destroyer of their beloved Country, which you were taught to abhor. You are a divider and a destroyer of America the beautiful.. .

THE CRISIS, by Charles E Miller, 6-23-10

POSTSCRIPT: Often in Congrssional committees and on-the-floorc caucuses about the costs of a bill, the language revolves not around the money so often as aroun the terms of the bill itself, the language in the bill. We we have in the White House a man whose history is alien to the history of this nation. His repertoire of language in such discussion contains not the same references as those of the mid-Westerner, the Souherner or Northerner. The word "cost" to the radical such as Obama has different references, in his mind, than does the word "costs" to a mid-Westerner. Therefore it is imperative that all bills be spelled out, the terms and language never taken for granted with this President. Much of his vocabulary and understanding of life he derives from radical Saul Alinsky and there neegade Karl Marx. Therefore, to comprehend what Obama plans, when he speaks, and when he has a plan it is necessary to structure his meanings in a way that promotes good communiation. Wealth to the Marxist may not mean simply moinetary wealth to the Continental American. Obama castigates CEO's of corsporations for flying about in their big corporate jets. This fixation derives not so much from the costs of the jet plne itelf as it does from the supposition that the costs of the plane and its use are derivitives of selfish enterprise, corporate acquisiton of assets stolen from other parts of the world, and la slingleminded deslireto pirate therest of theworld. In other world, wealth that ils global iby im;plicaions to Obama, the Marxist. The word "spread," the verb means to redistrib;ut;e the wealth of a few by way of its seisure by the ever growing Government, the very size of which is commensurte with the meaning of wealth to the Robinhood Marxist. \

PROFIT PLUS SPECIALIZATION,
A PRESIDENT IN DEFAULT

Citizen.

I saw at once in Obama's censure of profit in a post-campaign speech that promoted his health care plan and demonzied the insurance industry that such a censure belongs to his ideology. Karl Marx, Obama's mentor, denounced to the President's satisfaction that profit is the key to despicable wealth, personal and corporate, which in his fabricated socialist society must be spread about among all members of society. FAIRNESS in the redistribution of wealth, e.g.THE REWARDS FOR LABOR BY OTHERS is the guiding axiom of Obama's Marxism. Poor old Karl Marx! He felt so put upon by London's society, the Fleet Street bond makers and lawyers, the laborite enemies of a just redistribution of British gold! Lies, deceptions, trickery must not stand in the way of a just redisribution of wealth. . Barack Obama has proved the effective utility of these tools of satan, corrupts cions of the welfare State. Honesty in government is impossible while Barack Obama is in office. For him Republican capitalism is, in itself, a lie. His h age is to the "ruth" of Marxism and the omnivorous , gargantuan State with the power to suppress all aspects of profit i.e. capital invstment.

Many years ago, iln the 1950's, I reviewed a book for Joseph Henry Jackson of the book department at the "San Francisco Chronicle". The title of the book was THE ROAD TO SERFDOM, by Hayek. The book has since become a classic.. That was the pivotal point in my learning about a socialist economy. Therefore, I was prepared for Obama's ploy to eliminate profit by way of his health care plan, under his supposition--the Obama delusion-- that the absence of profit will "incentivize" the workers toil unjustly for the rich. The word "incentivize" is Obama's word for the destruction of this "unfair" hierarchy of CEO-Coroporate Management over sweat labor. .

PROFIT IS CAPITAL AT WORK , to be reinvested in the business or company or service, used to raise wages of employees and enhance the life-styles of all workers, above and beyhond their creation of a service or a product that attracts consumers. The formula is so simple! Thornstein Veblen's "onspicuous consumption," a spinoff of Marxism, is for Barack, not for the "workers of the world". He--as well as hiswife Michelle-- has proved he loves money and its affluent properties to the point of his worship of money. He, in fact, is a political engenue and disciple of Mollock, a biblical god of coin.

A socialist society is constructed on the supposition that wages only are sufficient for the workers, in satisfaction of their basic survival needs--to each according to his need. to all according to their ability. . Any enhancements must come from the Federal government in the form of entitlements That tyrannical control of private income of investment plus profits seized by higher and higher taxes for a "public industry" is the power Barack Hussein Obama seeks with his Obamacare bill. He does not give a damn about the sick the aged, the injured, the handicapped. He has proved over and over again that they are impediments to his career advancement insoifar as they block passage of his healh-care bill. His bill is so inclusive and controlling in the most intimate aspects of our lives that it, the health-care bill, will, realistically, destroy democratic America. What can be more humanly compelling than can our personal care for our health, intmate, sacrificial, urgent and non-negotiable? That is control. aside from control of one-seventh of our economy, our GNP.

Profit is money acquired by means of the involvement of customer, patron, client consumption of the offer of a service or product--beyond its cost to produce. He has never produce anything in his life for the market.   Obama covets for a gaggle of bureaucrats in DC that so-called "excess." He is convinced that that "excess" should go to the government instead of into the pockets of individual entrepreneurs and their workers. But why? you ask, given that that "excess" does not belong to the ontrol of bureucrats because they had no part in its acquisition   Envy, greed, lust for power, shame--all are factored in as reasons, Include gifts to buddies of Obama and his campaign supporters. (That is wy he is always in cmpaign mode...for the Mollock money inflow.) . He and his renegade disciples of Big Daddy Government claim that they are smarter than you and I and that thereftore his uses for that "excess" trumps your uses and are morally and pragmatically superior to your planned uses for that "excess." Barack Obama's only Presidential hope is that you will find happiness and contentment in your work without entreprenur profits, and that you will find increasing joy in working for wages only, without fringe benfits, bonuses, performance increases, job promotions or seasonal gifts, by order of the tyrant of the oligarchy, Barack Obama. Cheers! Try that on sycophantic professionals in all fields, tricksters of the Left in Congress and the Adminisrtration. The Media ;;have poved that Obama has what it tkes to make a great Presidency by outlawry. .

In the late 1950's I saw that the wealth created by profit above costs means affluence for the management and the labor of a company, for the individual businessman and his employees. The government under Karl Marx deplores that "excess," that income of consummer money that goes beyond costs. That excess creates the wealth he abhors, although, being a hypocrite, that wealth is an okay emolument for him and Michelle but not for Joe the Plummner. To eliminate worker and management profit in order to create better product or service is delusional. That is the chief delusion of socialism. It is the delusion Barack Obama clings to. European "workers of the world," peons, cannot envisiona a better life because that is the way they are raised, unlike Americans who will not settle for minimun i.e.Federally controlled wages. The Federal Government, with this administration, plays the people for fools because they, the people, cherish the concept of reward for labor in the form of money they can invest--and by which a consumer society flourishes. Omitting charitable impulses, what rewards other than money is there that you finely-tailord pieces of liberal political emptiness propose to the Congress as suitable for your worker-constituents? Paradise on earth? Utopia...of course, we capitalists should have guessed the answer. Mediocrlity in a trade-off with excetionalism.

The products and inventions and productivity in science, medicine, education are the envy of the world . Obama goes along with their envy and their hatred of America. He is ashamed of our opulence before the world and feels he must apoligize for our visible wealth. His shame we cannot help, since its origin is an old well-born codger in a London Library who invented work without profit as a way of life. Mr. Obama betrays his his ideological upbringing. The very stuff he b athes in, gambol in and accumulates for himself is the very stuff he curses as America;s shame.

But what the contemporary, outspoken liberal pundits omit is specialization. Peons possss no visible talents except for creating and breeding; the State prefers such abject submission by its serfs , its peasants, because thse mediocrities preserve the oppressors in power. On the other hand, the Doctor of Medicine says:-- I can make more profit by the practice of a speciality in medicine. The Engineer says:-- I can make more money building a better battery, a better prosthesis for medical use, a better dynamo for power plants, a better kind of kitchen ware for busy housewives, a better kind of GPS tractor, milking machine for daiymen...All are specialities designed and built by, and sold to meet consumers' special need. The engineers of these products are not driven to be fair in their profits; they are driven to make a profit in order to continue in their reearch. Obma considers such profitable research investment to be despicable and unfair. That is why he is an outlaw and a subversive enem;y of this nation.

Marx was an ignoramus about Western society's millions of special needs. Barack Obama 'is equally an ignoramus about 'American society's billions of special needs. He has the imgnation of a ground hog--only one burrow meets his career needs.."total transformation."

In his health-care bill, he woul reduce specialist doctors to general practitiioners, because he is essentially an ignorant man. You didn't know that. Many a university graduate walks across that stage knowing less than when he went in, matriculated is the word. His ;latent knowllede ils changed to reducio a d asudum; he hlas accepted the lberal-leftist preachments of his professors on many subjects, not lthe least of which is practitioner medicine. If he ils an English major, he will have learned ot discd Mark Twailn because in"Huckleverry Fim" Twain wites about a black man named Jim, ontheraft with H;ck to escape slavery. If he is a philsophy major, he wi ll have learned to discard Hobbes and Locke because they acknowleged the philosophy o economic growth by way of epresentative overnment and linvestment enterprise. No tenets of his capitalist upbrilnging will have survived; he will emerge as a convert to Mrxism disguised as the New Age outlok.

How does this shrinking of intelligent enquiry and common-sense wisdom occur--by de-information and, nowadays, by the almost universal doctrine on college and University campuses of political correctness. Obama's health care will destroy our great society of specialiation in all areas of life--the desireble absence of specialition will be exrapolated into, "deemed"useful to education, the insurance industry, corporate industries, banking! Why? Real substantive Specialization generates hideous profits. Our socity of the 21st century is too complex for the Marxian barter mindset. The Feds must radically curtail profit as an incentive and as a reality. Students will be bullied by the grading system into conformity lest they lose their Federal student loan! If Obama and his corrupt healthcare bill continue with a life of their own, this nation's great system of advanced education will surely deteriorate and become dismally mediocre with such special subjets being taugh as: "Exploring the Unisex," "Enhancing Your Biodata Card for Success," " Debt Reduction by Plastic Manipulation," "Spending 101," and "Gender Mnipulation for Economic Success."

Imagine, in banking--no specialization for a bank's consideration of loans! In order to promote an insipid, twisted and unworkable plan to make everybody equal\, regarless of talents or ambition or will, Obama would deliberately degenerate the brilliant innovations and humanitarian contributions of unique individuals by demonizing them as greedy, racists, out of touch wilth society e.g Federal policies of the New Age of Federal Enlightenment! No child is better at math than the next. No man has gifts that exceed the hopes of another. No leader is greater than any other leader in his vision, his abilities. All must be equal, must finish the race at the same time, cannot outshine another. Competition is harmful to the psyche of the loser, who thereby becomes a victim of a superior-performing, more talentd individual. That outlook is stupid , unreal, envious, retrogressaive to civiliation and an insult to the people. That sort of egalitarianism is to be imposed on profit-takers and on the creator-contributors, the inventors, the Edisons and the Wright-brothers and all the others who have contributed so profoundly to our society and to the wealth of the world at large. They have no right to fancy themselves superior in a world in which a tryant is trying to impose a false equality. Only the Narcissist in the Oval Offilce thinks comparatively. That's his sickness. Thjey thought in terms sf their invention and that only, not even its immense value to a civilized society!

This nation's wealth is created and invented, promoted, enlarged, made accessble to the world because of its emphasis on specialization. Men and women with special talents contribute to our society because of a specialization they wish to practice. Obama curses this specialization because it leaves out, by-passes himself and the Federal Government and leaves his small soul far behind, locked lin a bubble of self- admiration. He specializes in the destruction of free choice and the liberty to specialize--radical prohibiions layed down by the authority of the Communist Maniesto.

To you\ pundits I say--have your airtight case against socialism-- and Congatulatuions on thinking reaspms fpr "profit" through. Yet I supply the fool-proof padlock that, by the way, accommodates not just "profit takers." That padlock is SPECIALIZATION. Specialization explains all the myriads of inventions. It lis the common sense that produces a new product for the Market. I supply the chief cause for America's productive diversity--since diversity puts to use talents, as infinitely diverse as is Gods universe. Understand?

To President Obama, I say this:--that nothing in your agenda advances and encourages talents so much as specialiation. I think you became a community organizer, first, because you feared the adversarilal environment of the courtroom; then you sorrowed for the poor of East Chicago and you yearned to indulge yourself in the cronyism of your readical leftist mentors. Yet your self-love led you to think you were prepared to and destined by Peacher Wright's fairness god,to lead a great Nation--to adopt the ways of life of Stalin, Marx, Trotsky and Hugo Chavez, Tito , Breznev, King George III...(superior to our Founders) and force the American people by the example of these tyrants, to adopt socialism as a preferred way of life. That suppositious skewering of our two hundred and eleven year old practice of liberty, as a way of life, tells me something about the acuteness of your insight, your "vision," your lack of leadership ski\lls your failure to produce any product, cause, or goal in life for the people   Remove profit by law, and the gifted will refuse to invent, to improve, to explore, to contribute any longer. You will invite them to exercisetheir God-given gitfs like the Monks of the :Middle Ages. But you and Axlerod and Holder and Emanuel and your gang of surly, law-breaker advisors are too unaccountably too dumb to see the connection between profit and specialiation and an inequality of talents that generates true diversity and personally-rewarded ("incentivised") achievement.

Your singular and collective lust for power has blinded you to the true genius of America, its creative, inventive genius-contributions of the human imagination, the American spirit of hope and optimism born of the Colonial experience and the frontier life, the empathy of the American people for the imprisoned, the suffering of the world, a spirit driven by the hope of reward, in these instances of fulfillment of compassion's urgency, and then, when the test is material, such as landing on the moon, an America driven by the hope for, excuse me, profit to be realized, from the specialization-sciences of space exploration.

Profilt--reward--that derives from spcialization is the key and the lock to our productive , successful and affluent economy. It draws the world to us. Elinimate that interdependence and you, Obama, will sound the death knell for America's greatness, her springs of inventive genius and her generosity toward the rest of the world in their times of need. Go ahead, you Washington Democrat smart asses. Pass the health-care bill...but then it will be be too late. Then you will see that as a wise old man who has lived many years and has seen much, I am right on. The people? You have aleady damned the people by controlling them. You damn their basic "social contract," the US Constitution, by fabricating new laws and new offices without authority, by twisting and warping present laws to fit your feelings and the "political correctness" that substitutes for thought. By your supine benevolence toward the satanic governments of the world that envy this great Nation and its feeedom ways of life you weaken our defense. Defense of the people is the primary responsibility of the govenment and the Executive and the Commander-In-Chief of the armed forces. But before the world you curse our defenses as somehow insulting to those who would murder our people and trash our Country. You are, therefore, useless as President. You are a preposterous joke on the political scene, sir. It has taken them a a while to realize that they have been suckered in and made fools of, bu the people ae awake a last! They are not the great unwashed masses of your ignorant billing; hey ae not and will never become Europeanized Americans. You want it both ways, Barack Obama--an affluent life-style for yourselfandyour Saist disciples, yet. for the people, the denial of its honest validity in a free nation.

THE CRISIS, by Charles E Miller

POSTSCRIPT. At the time of this writing, the Unitd States is 14 trillion dollars in debt! That figure is incomprehensible to imagine It must not be raised any higher; we must face the prospect of naional bankrupcy. One Presidential candidate has suggested that that astononomical debt be distributed among the States, to let them repay as much as threy can, State by State. I am not certain. I do not know if, shold we empty Fort Knox, we woudl have enough gold to cover that debt. I know the Chnest hae their eyes on our gold reserves. Wemay act as uf we are free, but we are no longer a free people so long as we owe our lenders that sum of money. We may go through the motions of a free people, but we have been bought, due chiefly to Barack Obama's lust to spend taxpayer money. One man, a tyrant has put us in this position. Yet it is real, not illusory. W are slaves to that debt, as if the Chinese, the chief lender, has purchased us in the world's slave market to work in Chinest rice paddies. He conceals that relationship but attempting to distance us om our masters by he mention of taxes. As if our capacity to pay taxes liberated and disanced us from the bonds of that debt! Obsma's spending binge produced nothing of value to the American people. The Democats bought this about, the result of a one-party adinisration and Congress. Absolute power corupt sabolutely. We, the people, have been corrupted by the Democratic party's omnscience.

WANTON, IRRESPONSIBLE PRISONER RELEASE

Citizen.

The United States Supreme Court, by ordering the release of 46,000 felons from California State Prisons, has made itself the enemy of the people.

The ACLU that brought the case to the Court has again also made itself the enemy of the people

The 9th Circuit Court in San Francisco that issued the original injunction for release for cause by felons from State prisons is likewise the enemy of the people. All three agents have subverted the will of tlhe people and endageed heir lives, undermined the saey of our communities and shamed the notion that justilce upheld is justice honored. Think just of the hours spent in litigation that are trashed with this draconian release!

And liberal Justices Sotomayor, Breyer, Elena Kagan, Ginsburg and Kennedy--who wrote the decision--by uplding bad (9th Circuit) law, have made of themselves the enemies of the people. Their five to four decision demonstrated an unforgiveable contempt for the people of this State.

Their majority decision shows their unconcern for the consequences of the release of tens of thousands of felons. Their decision jeopardizes the safety, security, peace of law abiding citizens. And it, again, demontrates that government does not know how to handle crises, in this case the "overcrowded conditions" in the prison system, which presently accommodates some 145, 000 when designed to imprison 80,000. For how long have you meatheads in the system known this fact and mentioned it over tea to the devious kick-the-can squanderbums in Sacramento? Right. We elected them...our fault, partly. The growing excess must have been known b y Assembly men in Sacramento for ten yers...ten years to achieve that overcrowding of 46.000...perhaps longer.

Justice Scalia called the realease one of the most radical injunctions in this nation's history. The society of this State now stands in jeopardy as to their physical safety, the security of their property, the unspoken mandate for law and order essential to a harmonious social order. Just how are these releasees expected to survive outside of prison walls? ==es]ecp"ui ith so many in this and in other states out of work. A minority will, in fact pursue right conduct. Jobs or robbery? Work or theft? Fair play or shinanigans under the radar? Honest citizens or outlaws? Honest labor or drugs? Society must learn to accommodate, not to punish, criminals for their conduct. This release augers the breakdown of our justice system, at which time juries will become meaningless and, as in Europe, where a single politically-appointed magistrate makes decisions about guilt or innocence! Hail the politicization of jurisprudence in America!

The Court's selective release is yet another demostration of the amnesty mentality by the contemptous five, and but a step away from the destruction of law and order--anarchy. Who endorsed the release, what supernatural mind analyzed, forsaw and predicted success for these releasees? Magistrate, Sheriff, Bailiff, Jail Warden...who r evieweed the volum;inous case histories of each releasee to determine, like Zeus ex machina if he or she was a good rilsk outside prison walls? The jury system that put most of them there has become irrelevant with this maniacal release of California felons.

We must accept the assurances of "officials," who promise that the released prisoners, not parolees under the law, are not violent. Fools! What in hell does that promise insure? Kidnapping need no be violent, arson is not violent, burglery is not violentat at the time but may cause harm to the victim, larceny is intellectual, carrying a concealed weapon is not violent, drug-trafficking is not violent (a business transaction), fencing stolen property is not violent, unlawful real-estate property transactions are not violent...these are some of the offenses that do not require violence, as murder, rape and abduction. So what! This release constitutes an assault on society!

These czars of the system are devious in their reasoning away criminality and certain crimes as harmless to society because non-violent! We, the people, are enjoined to overlook the felonies of half a stadium-full of convicts and, by the radical, unconscionable concurrent decision of five liberals in black robes, accept a promise of harmless behavior by felons' turned loose upon us. I, as a citizen, hold those five in contempt of the people. Justice Kennedy should be removed from he bench for his endangerment to society.

The darling five of our highest Court have invented a new law: criminals can be forgiven (given amnesty) for their crimes providing they are good men and women without violent ambitions to repeat their offenses. New Law invented by Justice Kennedy. Amnesty shall be granted for felon convicts if they are the non-violent sort, based on their ;good bhvior while in prison." This is an omniscientaction of the State as God.

The worst consequence of this massive release is that it portends the POLITICIZATION OF OUR JUSTICE SYSTEM. Politics trump the law. Juries become irrelevant. A political appointee becomes the judge. Evidence is discarded. Sentences, as in this instance, are dissolved, expunged. A fair trial becomes an illusion of the past. ENTER SHARIA LAW to reconstitute justice. You blind, simple-minded, blaggards! I have nothing but informed, insightful, citizen contempt for the lot of you iln black roes, an you leser peddlars of faudulentjustice, including elecgd represeentatives of the people. Poppycock!. You in Sacramento could have done four things: (1) enlarged the present prisons; (2) shortened selected sentences; (3) converted cells into potties; (4) shortened prisoner terms by chain-gang labor on the deteriorting infrastructure.

Your reasoning is twisted and perverse, including that of the Court majority. You construe civility to mean accomodation by the law-abiding society. Arm yourselves for the assault on sobriety of conduct and lawful behavior. And don't, citizen Kennedy, give me that old bullshit about society not being perfect either. I must adjust to the possible robbery of my house or the jeopardy of kidnapping for ransom or rape of one of my daughters, or endure bottle-throwing mahem, requiring many police, and a lawsuit by the ACLU, enemy of the people, against the police for trying to quell the violence..

You have usurped our peace of mind, our security and our physical safety, arrogant gamester citizen Kennedy in a black robe. Justice Kennedy must think he is the forgiver, abettor of love, reassurer, savior of the felons from the discomfort of their crashed outhouses..

You., Majority of five, have forced us to join the felonious barbarians, whose saplent freedom without law you cannot possibly share, but indulge in liberation of criminals from their sentences despite your power to employ other solutions to overcrowding. Sure. Nobody wants a prison in his community. Present them, instead, with prisoners roaming about, jobless and now a part of our failing economy. Who knows the differencs in conduct between a jobless innocent citizen and a jobless former convict?

You and the other four usurpers have attempted to reason your way into morally right conduct on your part, and made of yourselves, you five in black robes, enemies of the people.

Secure your locks. Arm yourselves. Be vigilant at all times! Remember the bank and stagecoach robberies of the good old days. Pretend you are John Wayne. For this unimaginable, harmful move we shall pay dearly by the Supreme Court decision,

THE CRISIS, by Charles E. Miller

POSTSCRIPT: t\he United States Supreme Court has made anoher errors of judementto join--Taney's Dred Scott Decision, Pleney v. Fergusson...separate but equal. This will be ranked with those earlier faults in judgement aniimated not by a clear and honest discernment of the laws of natural rights but by personal vindictiveness. So it is with th sentimentl five who released 46,00 inmates, flawed thinking basd on personal opinion rather than the law. All prilsoners should have a place to crap and to sleep and when the situation seizes up, then they should be escused for their crimes and sent home like errant schoolchildren, into a free society where only the thin blue line of the police protects the citizens...and their own courage mustered to defend themselves and their familie with thier personal weapons.

POWER SEEKERS ABOUND

Citizen;

I derive many of following truths and concepts from Rousas Rushdoony's book "Christianity and the State." Consider this letter a book review of Dr. Rushdoony's very excellent and enlightening exposition of the hostility of God toward the un-righteous State...The Godless State, a theocracy not otherwise to be inferred. My contribution is the appliation of his concepts. Romans 13 predicates a righteous State, God's secular agent and minister, that operates within God's will, the which evil-doers should fear when they fail to "subject" themselves to the righteous State, that is, to obey the laws of their society. I linterpret Romans 13 to refer to an ideal state, ceated and governed by imperfect men.

That was the State envisioned by America's Founders. Their vision was not a thleocracy but a secula State whose leaders respeced the law, honored God and practiced honest dealings with the people. Our leaders today envision a secular, globalist God-denying State that excludes the faith of our forefahers, eliminates God from schols, public forums and State recogniton while at the same time, they admit satanist worship as legitimate relgious worship in the military, expung the name Jesus: from the ministries of all chaplains. TheState is today ready to punish teachers and scholchildrenfor anyexpression of TheChristian faith ithe classroom, not eventoadmit ofilts historicity in olonial times.

The "completely transformed" State moves intransformation from liberty to oppression, from individualism to masses conformty, from enterprise to submission, from opportunity to Statist regulations, from productivity to entitlement, from enterprise to obedience, allthese changes contemplated by Marxist disciple Barack Obama. Radical Obama is currently hoping to acquire total power, disguised as relativstic compromise with our history and our laws, a dictatorship of the Presidency. To this end, Obama, Pelosi and Reid have arrogated sovereignty, disguised as bi-partisanship, unto themselves/ Thistrip has found it expedient to trick the people into acceptance of Obamacare without a legitimate House vote on the Senate bill for Obamacare. The House voted onthe"fixes " to the actual bill, which nobody had read. The actual bill was passed as a "rider," like a funding amendment on a usual piece of legislation. The vote was for a "reconciliation" of the Senate bill the Senate bill being "deemed", or rauher presumed" to have passrd...Tricky, no? Dishonest is the proper word tod escrie this manipulation of the law. Without a hand-count ofthe House vote for theSenate bill, the legislation was not lawfully passed from the Senate tothe House of Representatives. To "deem" a bill as having passed is a substitute for an actual vote on a bill, the text of which must remain unchanged and identical when transmitted between the two Houses. To "deem" is not to vote. To deem is to presume agreement and that is fraud of a major piece of legislation. Passage was, therefore, outside the control of the US Constitution by the abusive use of House rules!. The House rule of presumpion is not intended as an irresponssible asubstitute for actual hand-count passage. The one-party Congress seemed to be content with the deception.

By using this device, which changes one-sixth of the US economy, the Congress usurps. abuses, oversteps the Article I powers given to tlhem by the Constitution, which has total sovereignty to fix and to control the course of this nation of laws. "The Constitution! Perish the Constitution! We"ll devise anothe Constiutional convention that will shift the balance of power our way! Give it life!" radicals scream...what a ploy to avoid reality Reaity? Americans have yet to experience the destructive costs of the deemed Obamacare bill.

To suggest that God plays a role in our government sounds irrelevant to the pragmatic matter of Constitutional passage of the legislation. I am not silent as to the ultmate consequences, but I say, at this time, that such a device of trickery--the House can make its own rules--augers the destruction of a nation by default. We will all suffer in that destruction, which will result from the " transformtion" through a piratical seizure by the White House scheme. What else can you call boarding the car industry and with sabre flashing, tearing contractual laws into sheds? All three boarding pirates of the Regime were involved in the fraudulent deemed "passage" of the Obamacare bill. They were in fact, the conspirators of a despicable fraud against the people.

Do you see any humility in their magisterial words to control the people by fraud and precedural manipulation? Small wonder Obama demeaned "process." Obmacare was "passed" by a deception of the people Be aware that when the State by example, choice and ignorance eliminates God's providence from its customs, values, laws and traditions, it becomes the source not just of all power but of counterfeit ethical and moral virtue. Replaciln the Creator appealed to the the Declaration of Independence, the State hss become like God. Its actionns become vrtuous and final and absolute. The State has then empowered itself to enforce conformity and uniformity in the cause of ethical "fairness." The virtuous State, without any other reference than itself, can then deterine the kind, extent and expression of its own power.

The State ean do no wrong.

That is Washinton's attitude today. Those given un-Constitutional powers, as the 39 Czars and the cabal of stooges for Obama, will autocratically and alone, judge what is and is not "fair." Because it is absoluely virtuous, the State will determine what is criminal, wrong, unjust and illegal and thus thus the government in DC, conrolled by fallible men, will establish its closed system of humanistic values in which man is the center. The State is then. by its own self-declaration--qualified by judicial consent to try war criminals as civilian lawbreakers with its perfect justice. There is no higher power. The State becomes the source of virtue. Churches, religion, home schooling are all irrelevant and must be allowed to atrophy in the New Age of globalist America.

Dishonesty is virtuous when the means justfy the end. Freeing prison inmates is virtous if the act will balance the budget. Taking from one man, his home, his business to give to another citizen--by eminent domain without domanic values--is virtuous if that other "needy" person lacks a home, a business, a hard-working income or a public enue such as a mall. . This transfer of wealth is called an entitlement by the radical preent Admlinistration. The seizure of private property to give to another private person becoes a virtuous act in the eyes of the virtuous State. It is virtuous politically to brainwash kids in the grades by White House videos because those kifd will later become productive socialist citizens as a result of having been brainwashed to to think like string marrionettes and to produce for Uncle Sam.

It is virtuous to destroy the notion that captal is wise, prudent, advangtageous, and risky, because capitalism is anathema to fairness in a democracy where all are equal. It is virtuous to control medical doctors but not trial lawyers, because the benefits to the former are rooted in greed but the trial lawyers practice a degree of fairness in their canons and causes of action that benefits all of society. Whereas a surgery may be botched--the false fear behind lack of tort reform in Oamacare in a trial for equity of care aganst the doctor or the hospital brings rewards to the deprived patient claimant. That is the politicization of medicine. That is "fainess" in action. As the sole souce of virtue, again, the State can therefore do no wrong.

As its powers increases, the State's zeal to penalize dissent increases.

We see that today, wherein a Senator will attempt to cut off dissent by punishsment against the dissenter or his agent in one form or another. We see that today in the cowardly silence of the media to expose Washington retributon against dissent. Penalties can consist of jail, fines, illicit (expedient) taxes, disdainful laugher by the President, mockery of the people and denegration of the nation's history. These are all devices of the tyrannical State. It is morally wrong to replace the courts and legislatures with violence and open revolution. It is expeditious to see the benevolent Rulers focused on expanding government power in order to control the people's lives and, according to Marx, spread the unjustly-acquired wealth not just to Americans but to the resj of the "suffering" world. Obama, like Marx, haes capitalism; he cosiders our exceptional scoiety and thrivingculture to e the result, generally, of a nation of paasites. He hates the American people for this reason and cause. He, therefore, feels compelledto enfoce Marxism; on Americans. They will become the slaves and willing victims to this process of change. when they accept theState as their sol benefactor. Propaganda! Already, the mainline media are literally the propaganda arm of the Obama administration.

Barack Obama is attempting to create a class- society of controllable workers for and under the heel of the government as receivers of the government's largesse. I am convinced that he intends to crush the wealthy and middle-class into one, undefineable mass of entitlement recipients, docile before the new god of the State, and happy and contented to receive the provisions of a central government that is evil in its intent and pratices. I'm waiting for a Minister of Information, a Goebbels of propaganda, to emerge and be named an Information (Propaganda) Czar. Is it already the Press Secretary?

By making their authority absolute, the Rulers become an abomintion in God's eyes. They usurp the will of a righeous people, in complete contradistinction to Romans 13, that promises a righteous government and an obedient people who need not fear the State unless they do evil. Without God the State is the determiner the boundaries , extent and appliations of its own power. According to Romans 13, the State is the minister of God. When , however, the State presumes to be our material and implicitly our spiritual savior, it transgresses God's law and becomes evil. Salvation from what? From needs, from the injustice of wealth-seekers, and from the "unfairness" inherent in our history. When, in effect, the State becoms the total provider of our human needs, it usurps God's role in human intercourse and practices evil; (God! Ask God for food stamps!) The government becomes evil when the State promotes its salvic power, salvation from evil, salvation from death, salvation from immoral acts...as defined not by Scripture but by the corrupt will of the Marxist State Courts and the rulings of a manipulted Supreme Court. Gone will be conscionable acts by the government and by the people. Gone will be true justice but rather. in its place, the advent of a mediocre society in education, medicine, business and local administration. Gone will be the competiion that elevates an exposes supriority in work, product and ambition.

At this point the State replaces the church, replaces religious faith and establishes itself as the arbiter of morality, virtue and justice and ,without God, becomes the inventor of laws to suit its own will. That is anarchy. A man has the right to the fruits of his own labor? No, the State has that rght--Obama's State-- and, seizing those fruits, he will redistribute them according to its, his, doctrine of "fairness." That is Europe's godless, mediocre and unproductive environment.

The State, i.e. government is God's agency for the welfare not of the Rulers but of the people. Thus Obama's agenda is for the welfare of the Rulers--leftists, trial lawyers,National union supporters, lobbyists. enjoyers of taxpayer bailout emoluments--and not for the welfare of the people. The Government, i.e the State is today a Godless entity. We can, therefore, expect it to lie to us, to cheat on the people, to innovate laws that break the Constitution, to seize powers delegated to the other branches, to indebt the people for four gerations and by trickery and obfuscation eventually wipe out the Bill of Rights thereby, purging persoal freedoms in the bill of Rights, while ultimately destroying our great country. The cowardly silence of the "free press" is a Federal indulgence. The media no longer has a soul. They re a ridiculous joke. "Truth, what s ruth?" the media ask, like Pontius Pilagte at Christ;s trial. Truth is what Barack Obama says it is. N'est pas?

Man was not created in the image of the State but in the image of God. Therefore Barack Hussein Obama is first answerable to God. As the State, the usuper dies--that despite all signs to the contrary--man's responsibility for his actions and his freedom will increase. For there comes the death of freedom whenever man becames god. The modern humanistic State is a jealous god and will tolerate no contending rivals. Indeed, it indulges in immorality (see lies, scandals, back-room deals, bribed votes in Congress, broken promises, colossal selfishness in government, heartless acts of closure agaist the citizens with job and housing losses) The State will tolerate no moral declarations, actions or presumptioms of independence and individualism among the people under its control. The traditional American individual in all of his copious expressions of personal pride, is the natural enemy of the State. In fact license given to imoral acts, as plunderingingof t he txpayers, by the State's subtle, unspoken sanctions engenders a fear from which the State promises protection. Thus we will witness the growing tolerance for immoral conduct among the citizens as a means of Statist fear-control.

Accompanying that tolerance for immorality among the popuace comes an increase in taxes to control them--a fraud-- and a lessening of true government alongside ever-increasing illicit power. When a State becomes prophetic of the future, it assumes the role of Jesus Christ and the church. As the State becomes more powerful, it increases its pressures to conform and to nforce uniformity in conduct, acquissition and Veblem's "conpicuous consumption."...in today's language--to be fair. It is politically-correct to endorse a mindless "fairness," but nobody knows exactly what it means! To give awards to people who have not earned them? To make sure that no family has to make a sacrifice greater than anotherin or to have a successful marriage, to acquire an education...? Fools! Obama's attempt to "transform" America into a Utopian nation of enforced equality will bring this nation crashing down economicaly. We are not all equal, Charlatans.

Note: that with the increase in power comes less true government (benevolent abstention, cautious intervention, "careing" regulation) and more taxes. We are in that broiler today. Obamacare is not governmen at its best. It is Statist compulsions through taxes to benefit the bureaucrats and leftists in the administration and in the Congress. The goals of the authoritarian State are control, regulation, jurisdiction and power. The control is established in order to authorize the Rulers to manipulate the economy and all institutions that contribute to that economuy. With that control comes the power to invent new laws, break the basic Constitutional law, judge the citizens without charges and usurp power from existing branches of government. \

Obama legislates, Obama silences the court and invents (legislates) Czars with (autocratic) powers not granted to them by the Constitution. He is, in effect, an outlaw in charge of the government, smirking at and mocking the people who put him there. He is a fraud, an incompetent, a radical manipulator, a ne'er-do-well from Chicago's manchine politics. He promotes disharmony in order to justify invented-law changes in government. His 39 Czars bathe in invented powers over the people. Talk about legislating from the bench! Barack Obama legislates from the oval office!

When the State becomes a terror to good men, it has ceased to merit obedience. (Rushdoony) l repeat. When the State becomes a terror to good men, it has ceased to merit obedience. Remember that. And when under these circumstances religion is merely tolerated, it is not free. It is allowed to exist by fiat, condescension, tolerance of the all-powerful State. Religious fith, selected chuches are therefore subject to removal, cancellation and condemnation by the State. Belivers in God ecomethe radicls to the true radicals ofthe left.

As the salvationist State becomes the agency of providence, it replaces God. When the State can do no wrong, the citizen's freedom is illusory. Under these circu;mstances of the inculpability of the State, the citizen has no right to differ with the State, that is, to differ by any attempt to oppose a provision that has been secrely embedded in Obamacare, as the Biodata card. It bears repeating that when the State acts to replace God in the minds of the people, it becomes the providential replacement for God to control the actions and especially the thoughts of the people. In short, resistance is made to appear unfair, unlawful, and anti-social--the croaking of the Leftists--because individual thought as a matter of dissent is contrary to the "wisdom" of the State. All resistance is therefore hostile to the omnipotent socialist State, regardless of what the Conservative-traditonalist resists. Dissent is made to appear seditious! In order to insure "fairness", ths State exerts pressures for conformity, compliance and uniformity. At that critical j;uncture in the deteioration of freedom, responsinble expressions of honesty by Rulers of the all -powerful State exist no longer, nor are they necesary for the ruleship of the Elites. No longer under anyu; a;u;thority from God and his gifts of life, liberty and the pursuit of happiness, the people become a human utility of th4 state; their very numbers assumes the nature of expedient eistence for the benefit of the State, serfs, in other words, to the Elites., this metamorphis of total transformation a ssisted by the demand by theState and its folower, its civil disciples of politial -correctness Adoration of the State and is Rulers becomes politically-correct in all vnnues of public expression, including the pulpet.

Therefore bald-faced lies are permitted in order to advance and to enlarge the State because lies are useful to the promotion of ever greater power control of the people. Again, the end justifies the means. By ruling out God in public discourse, by attaching fines to expressions of faith in public throught, and by trivial court rulings, Christians are singled out and punished.as the ever-growing State asserts its humanistic, absolute power. In order to legitimize Obama's lies as truth, the State is compelled to consider the common people as stupid and ungrateful and, as a shibboletlh of Marxism , they, Amerians, will become the illiterate (European) " unwashed masses."

Our ignoramus-of-history President is a consummate liar. His words and his actions are not to be trusted. It follows then that to legitimize his lies about his agenda, he literally must in his absolute authority--by his actions--transgressive of God, consider the people as incapable of caring for themselves. Therefore, he urges us, the people, to thank him as god--a whimper he has expressed in his most recent dishonest judgement. I say again, that he is not to be trusted either his words or his actions. Having grown up in Hollywood, I was innoculated against his smiley, smooth-talking sort of charisma and seachlilght movie-set glitz. I honestly believe that my highschool educaion in the 1940's excels his collegiate training at Harvard!. I learned the value of character and the meaning of truth-search and I learned to think. He has learned none of these. Karl Marx, Saul Alinsky and his leftist piratical crew do the thinking for him. Leftist Idealogue Obama offers opinions as searching-thought to the people. He is danerous because he is likeable and clever. like a pretender to the king's throne, in a word, Machievellian...agreeable in a platitudinious manner of speaking. Cheers!

THE CRISIS, by Charles E. Miller 7-21-11

POSTSCRIPT: There is no explantion for men's lust for power to control a natoin of free peole,excep the impetus of political station, the will of satan within the human heart and the diabolital lust to be as gods. Thas been ever thus down through human history; it is no diffrent in the America of the preset Adinistration, a diabolital cabal of power-greedy men, elected yet withot the conscience to follow the law or the character to execute the will of the people.

RAISE THE DEBT LIMIT

Citizen.

To raise the debt limit is the way to conceal waste, earmarks, squanderous entitlements and laundering corrupt money in the process--or else we shall lose our fiscal status as a solvent nation and be unable to meet our obligations, domestic and global in the repayment of borrowed money. That status is known as going into default..

And whose fault is that...Outlaw Barack Obama and his congerie of highwaymen in the Admionostration and in the Congress ie. librals and leftists who are convinced that this nation's prosperity is the result of parasitism on the poor of the world. We Capitalist Americans are the cause f their poverty...the devil's spittle on our honor.

The way to creative prosperilty is blocked by a gang of cuthroats and ignorant whippersnappers who want to control our journey. We can handle the loss of reputation; we refuse to forgive or to overlook the squander of a grng of sychopnant thieves and millious of liberal dogooders. Get out of the way, you statist men and women without wisdom or valor triumphant in disguise...we know who you are--Obama and his Adminisrative advisors, czars, liberals and lefists in the Congress. Our exceptional country is proof of what God's laws of natural rights can accomplish. Name one people from whom Americans have sucked the life blood of prosperity, endangeed their ways, their health, or profitted from their povertyand hardship. Our history shows just the oppossite. You lying fools persuade no one without common sense and understanding and even a slight knowledge of our samaritan history..

You see but you do not believe what you see. That response is called stupdity, out of which which you have invited and, or accepted the colossal poitical failure of socialism and its denial of the image of God. All en ate not equal in their endoments yet are equal before God as His creation. This nation has grown great because of variety amongst human beings, enjoying those natural rights that come from God, the liberty to invent without regultions, and a created prosperity unmatched by any other nation with whom we share the world. We are the most generous and wealth expending nation on the planet, you dangeorus, intractible oppressors of the power-jungry left.

Impugn Obamas as an outlaw for good reasons. He has crashed two car maiufacturers, scorning investors and business contracts and CEO reponsibiteis He has taken over banks, manipuated the currency citizens, a move in itself an act of treason. He is contemptuous of the Constitution; it stands in his way. ; His solution is to subvert Constutional laws into politca;l stratagems. Barack Obama is not just an outlaw; he is also a subversive.

He has paid off his voters and supporters in the Federal Unions, set up a coterie of 40 czars to do his marxist bidding, unseen. He now forms a panel of 26 experts to oversee the "stupid public " of over 300 million citiens. Think of the megalomania behind that establlshment!

These are but a few of his broken promises, sly violations and radical misinterpretations of of the law and gut-rotting machinations during his term in office. He has earned the status of a candiate for impeachment, having commimtted numerous misdemeanors and treason durin his two and a half yeas in office.

Those who are still on his side are ignorant of American history and are totally consumed by his entitlement programs...free food, free housing, free citizenship!. We risk the riots in the streetsi if entitlements are cut...a fear of the liberals.
greece is the example of social spoilation.

We the people do not deserve what will follow refusal of the Congress to raise the debt ceiling. But we are tough customers , resilient, innovative, and peranently enemies of Obam[s marxism.

Our stage coach stands resting, the team is restess, snorting, with the hill of time ahead.

Get the hell out of the way, you gang of highwaymen and supporters with"Press" in your hatbands. You're blocking the road. The whole lot of you belong in jail, as desperadoes, breakers so the fundamental law, co-conspirators, highwaymen who lust for power that you demean yet deny to the common people through their Representatives. Were this a balefield of invaders,which is your mission, to ivade the rights of the common citizens of this great Republic, this country,we would take you out one by one as we did the British king's redcoats. That shows the level of hatred and disgust we conservatives hold your corrupt machinery in Washsington DC. Buzzards that hoover over econmic and optimistic death!

Hyah...!" The whip cracks, the lead team plunged into their hardness and the coach moves on torward ts detimatio, a amall distant government and much open road of a renewed America ahead.
`Again, Barack Obama, you are an outlaw and your gang of worshippers share in your outlawry.

THE CRISIS, by Charles E..Miller 6-26-11

POSTSCRIPT; To raise the debt limit involve not only the fraud, disguises of fraid. threats of economic collapse. and trillions more in free spending   To transfer from the lower House their Article I,Section 7 to borrow is, unllawfully ,   to transfer a constitutional power to the Executive to borrow money, a power strictly accorded to the House of Reprpesentatives (Article I, Sec. 7) The Foumnders put this limit on Executive power for a reason: the House of Repesentatives is closest to the will of the people as theyir local Representtives, and therefore they are answerable to the people...whenthey go home for recess. . The President is not directly responssible to the people. His job is sto Execute legilation, not to create it. .

More eimportantly, the Separation of Powers into three branchs--Executive, Legislative and the Judicial--demands that only the lower House borrow money and raise money through taaes. Those responsibilities are restrcted to the House of Representatives...restriced by law. There is no option. For the President, even on one occasion and because of desperate circumstances to borrow money, wilhout the power Constitutionally to do so, and apart from any power held by the lower Houe, to grant the President that authority is to set a precedent for a future dictator who can an will blankrupt the American peopl in order to to etablish his power, to intimidate the people, to crush the American spirit of enterprise and to show the an envious world his contemp for American Capitalism. If Obama exercises the 'umawful power to raise the national debt, he sets that precedent. He forever joins the Executive to the Legislative-powers--disregard the irrelevant blatlherskyte of past instances of debt-limit raisings-- he has usurped, robbed the Congress of an office and a powerthat is theirs alone, by law.

Let's go further.   If the President unlawfully raises the debt limit, unilatgerally, by borrowing more trillions of dollars, he will impoverish the nation by exacting from its people tax money in excess of their Gross National Product figure. His bankrupcy of a formerly exceptional nation will lead to all sorts of fraud, deception in government, distrust of our leaders ,chaos and riots in the street, as in France and Greece, , and the national suicide of a once great nation. As Ben Franklin said, if the people want to becomeslaves, they wil become slaves.

FROM MAUDLIN TO MASTER

Citizen

Even the cutworm changes, the silkworm goes through its cyclic changes, the poitician, pretending to side with have-nots, goes through his amorphic change of remorse by pretending to share low-liness with the discontented in the country. Barack Obama is like the king's fool who mimics disaster to demonstrate his superior brainpower majesty to the liberals and to agitate the common people to panic or intimidation or insecurity--all to the destruction of freedom and the suppression of "danerous" innovaion of the political opposition. He believes that Americans frighten easily; he the boogymanof capitalism's impending disasters , whatever they may be...such as climate change (climate has changed for six billion years), , electricity shortages, demon coal and satanic oil..... That is his radical quid pro quo stratedy-to alarm the people with a fictional crisis, yet camly entreaties them to ttake his side of an issue. The Media perceive Obama as a prophet, messiah, scientist, truth-bringer and revolutionary of sorts. He dlispoes of America's history as il it were garbage and lhe can do so wilth impunty because he has the mdia's support and he believes not in America's past. He has never, ever sacificed anything of himself for this Repulic. He has bcome a maudlin parasite who embraces our enemies and fawns upon our allies.

Power lies not in his words but in his actions. To the extent that he appears to be a regular guy, he catches his opponents, the enemy, off guard. His strategy is to condemn his minor faults in an orgy of self-criticism. Barack Obama is good at this. He goes only so far as the to entice the liberal media to agree with him. They are his arm of propaganda, worthless in a free society but instruments of power to keeping Obama as king. They are, however, deluded to think that they are free to give their liberal opinions as unbiased comment or honest news reporting. In fact, they are condescending toward Obama and even more so now that he is in office. This tactic does not fool shrewd conservatives, for they link the media; hypocrisy to the shallow contempt of President Obama for those Americans who have focused their lives on wealth, the curse of our society, according to the President. President Obama is a chameleon.

But let us go further. Senator Obama practiced his radical Olinsky strategies while in the Senate, voting "present" a hundred times to conceal his radical posture, voting against big business, the sacredness of life, although he approves China's successes at purchasing American shares in industry and is silent bout the attacks onChinese Christians and the abence of human rights in that communist country.

Watch his actions, he sides not with the radicals of the left but seems to move politically further center as he encounters hawks andeaparty patriots. This shift is an a deliberate, practiced illusoruy maneuver, accomplished by his seeming to be concilliatory with the capitalist clique in Washington, and disarming to political illiterates.

He is a competent magician at creating political illusions, a gift that won him the Presidency. He ils not what he seems to be, a reasonable, concilialtory politician rather than an iron-fisted demagogue. He deludes the opposition into believing, at least partially so, that he is ,what he wants to be --on their side, but that the realities of (illusory) circumstances (Great Depression Crisis, diseased millions,etc.) prevent him from taking a convincing biparftisasan role in things like health care, nationalization of the banks,car makers, insurance companies, energy industries, deception of the Media.

He has worked his"wicked will" (Churchhill) by sustaining the proposition that most of American demands a change from the Bush administrations years. Actually, it could be a little more than 50 percent of America, and that can be further trimmed by Obama's egregious solicitation s to mock our history...impugning our motives to increase this nation's prosperity.

In a nation whose youth are dismally ignorant of our history, it is a fools trick to turn their minds into channels of dissatisfaction amounting in some perons to a hatred of our way of life, which features contentment with an imperfect Republic and democracy.

He intends to prove that any that liking for the American way of life is ill=founded, unfair to the rest of the world, radically unjust and destined to destroy most of us with disease, poverty, hardship and malcontentedness. Barack Obama hasn't a clue about our pioneer spirit that rought life to this nation out of the wilderness. He is an alien to our history. What has Barack ever suffered? Nothing, and therefore he expects us to condemn our cultural history by his words. He is not euipped to know by experiences. Instead, he knows by ideology, alone.

THE CRISIS, by Charles E..Miller

POSTSCRIPT: BaackObama underestiates th spsiritual strengthand brilliant inventive capacity of Americans. We are, indeed, a nation of inventorsWe linventeddiffeent sorts of shvels for different tasks. We invented the light bulb, thautomobile,thairplane, aspilrin andtothpaste. We ilnvented thestop watch, thespace shuttle and matches. And...onand on.
What the pioneer settler needed by way of a tool, he linvented andhammeed out on his forge. ILn Oama's lexicon, we stoled these thngs fromthe rest oftheworld, includingtheir wealth and industry. That ideological lie has given rise to his illusion that we are a nation of economic and cultura parasites. That presumption leads one to conclude that he not only misunderstands the American people; he hates them aswell. Yet he hides his hatred behind

sllken speech, eloquent but empty platitudes and non-involving everyday observations. Who can disagree that millions of Americans are out of work? He thinks hmself to be an adroit observer and profound investigator of the American scene. He is a drone.

Yet he is our precious little bundle of nonsense whom we must endure for another year and more. God only knows that his Marxist ideology willl conjure up for him to guide a free people. Can he be so blind and dumb, in the intellectual sense, that he does not see the cause for the calamitosus state of our economy. my answer lis "yes." It's hard to believe that a Harvard grad can be so mentally inert and perceptively blind that in the midst of an eocmoomic crisis he finds his golf game a more challenging activity for the moment. Yet his obsequeous maudlin embrace of our enemies has its limits. Those overtures were disgusting. Now, become the Master of the castled in DC, and having broken the basic law of the land the Constitution, myriads of times for his career benefit, we are now faced with a Master who is consumed with envy of the rest of the world. He would like to possess it, I strongly suspect that after his swift departure from Washington, he will gravitate toward the United Ntins, one of the bellwethers of his administration.

FRAUD IN THE MISSING) BUDGET

Citizen.

We are " fortunate" to have constitutional lawyers in the House who are competent to decide issues within their jurisdiction. What category of jurisdiction, Mme Speaker?   Jurisdiction in rem, in peronam, subject matter, Federal and State, original, pendent. Which does the good dame mean?

The blank cheque statement is worthless before the oath to support and defend the constitution of the United States.   Under Articie I, Section 8, clause 18, The Congress has the power " to make all Laws whch shall be necessary and proper for carrying into Execution the foregoing Powers and all other Powers vested by this Constitution in the Governmen of the United States or in any Depart ment or Officer thereof."

Question: Where is the implication or command or constrained liberty of advice appertaining to the healthcare welfare of the entire people either denoted, suggested, demanded or implied in this clause of the Constitution? I an a literate citizen, and I cannot find it.

Therefore, logic and reason and common sense oblige me to declare that the use of legislative power to compel citizens to take out health insurance--whether from both houses or one only--is improper, unlawful and un-Constitutional. The Constitutional jurisdiction granted by said body of laws does not impower either Congressmen or Senators to invent a supra-power that is not granted by the nation's basic body of laws.

You covet the power to conrol what is most vital and sensitive to the people--their personal health.   You criminalize non-compliance by your denial of free choice. and your threats of imprisonment. What if the youth cannot afford either the $3,800 fine or the cost of a jail term and additional fine? You would impose medicare edits that are injurious and destuctive to freedom in America. Your lust for oligarchial command that we shall conform is evident in the bill you present.

You do not understand it, nor will the people. Yet you thrust upon 300 million individuals the contempt for our present system, which we find adequate, all the while ensconcing your colleagues in the law--the trial lawlyers--in readiness to debase the Constitution, defraud the people of the truth about our care, and crush the life from the general citizenry with court penalties based on your ill-gotten notions of justice. In short, you plan to encourage tria lawyers to grow fat upon the carcusses of medical practitioners, and who, like buzzards, will never be satisfied. This curse of darkness you intend to visit upon the American people with your Obamacare, you soulless giants of disesteem and pilgmy intelligence,Reid, Pelosi and radical leftists in both Houses of the Cogress. You assume a station of superior lintelligence that is demonstrated neither by your words nor your actions. Your dull small minds and corrupted intentions will destroy the gifted in this great Republic. You radical leftists in the Congress are a lden of vipers!

Those laws, by the way, ladies and gentlemen of the Congress, were made solely for the proteciton of the people from oppressive and destructive and unlawful use of power of oficials in office, the which you repesent. You are certainly not the British parliament of 1776. The US Constitution was not constructed for the benefit and aggrandizement of sitting officers, howsoever wdl intentioned. I say this cum laud. I am a student of men as well as of the Constitution. And, besides being a grauduate of Stanford, I am the published author of 30 books. " l am your huckleberry".
""

What are those foregoing Powers and all other Powers vested by this Constitution in the Government of the Unted States or in any Department or officer thereof? Do they suggest that Congreessmen are not to trust the people? Do those powers mock over two hunded years of our brilliant history of struggle and enerprise and freedom? Do such allege outside-the law inventions cancel out pleadings by the oppo]sition that, to wit, the healh care (and other monsterous legislation) is destructive to this nation? Indeed, do your privae practices as lawyers intrude upon your good judgement as elected officials? That I suspect is the case. We will, in fact, tell you arrogant sheisters how to run your office, and if you find this depresses your egomania and infringes upon your will to control the people, then get out and good riddance. More civic-worthy men and women will replace you. Wait until medical-care desperation sets in. Humiliy is not your Zeitgeist. leftist pretenders.

To Mme Pelosi. I say that empowerments of " original" and/or of " pendan"t jurisdictiosnal control by House members, regardless of their legal education, is worthless, irrelevant and unlawful. They are gratuitous emoluemnts of her --anr Reid's--radical chosing. The Speaker of the House does not possess that " original" power, especially when standing before the last clause quoted above. She has not the authority to concockt a power and then to bestow that power upon any Congresman or Congresswoman, like a royal Madam Queen of the kingdom. She thereby emboldens them with a jurisdictional aura they do not possess in generality. For the Constitution is very selective and narrow about its distribution of powers. I does not emoulate Congress with Parliamentary discretion to make any law lawful. (Parliment tried that with the Stamp Tax, thr flint that ignited the powder of our Revolution. Britons against Brttons.)

It was delibaretly designed in order that the people, fugitives from similar oppressive mercenaries in Europe, might live in freedom, the freedom to make their own choices about what is most intimate to them, their medical care. Have you ever heard of the plague, the black death, about the lack of standards of sanitation and cleanliness, about bleeding to cure a disease, about phoney medicine called "elixirs of healing, about hypnosis healing, about healing magic, charlatans (Magi) of medicine and taking the cure in waters, and more ? Obamacare would return to this country some of these delusions of good medical care! Like phoney medications,quackery treatment and the lack art of political persuasion that Uncle Sam is taking care of you and your children. for their entire lives.

Trusting in God as they did for their welfare and their survival, that includes good health, they fled old vassal-state Europe. Imitating the prince of deception, our President would turn you to imitate fading old Europe by his collaborationist (leftists in Congress) elimination of enlightened medicine in the United Statges. Why do you think people from all over the worldc ome to this country for diagnosis and teatment with the finest doctors, nursing care, practiced medicine, pharmaceuticals and supporting devices, not to mention clean, top-of-the-line hospitals and secondary help, such as therapy, follow-up care, devices supply--no waiting slx ;moths fo crutches--and brilliant advice. Huh? You lobsters of underover. closed -door, surreptitious and therefore criminal changes,change chanes tht are derived toadvance careers, enrilchCongressmen, sustain the corrupt statusquo of Washington potitics and pauperize the people wilth generational debts in the trillions. Youa are mad, you socialist demons ofl hell, mad. Do you hear me? Retro-growth? Let me be clear: Barack Obama did not appoint you to represent him. Are you also Czars? You were eleced to represent the people. My fine mind grasps the differences.

Furthermore, we who will be the allegd "beneficiaries" of said bestowal have a right to reject that power because we are neither subjects of the Obama crown, nor are we vassals of the Federal governmen State. If we do so, let it be said that we --not all conservatives, by the way--rebel with intelligence and comprehension. We are citizens under the baslc law of the land, the US Constitution.

No Congressperson has an inherent right to override the circumscribed power of his or her office in order to effect a law by fiat, a change in a law wlithout debate (we've seen non substantive debate on the Obamcare bill(s) NoCongressmancan, without majority passage, add a provision to a law, stipulate an uauhoritative to be followedconsqeuence of a law, give a statutory replacement interpretation of a law, render personal application of a law, devilse new law without debate (as 1,017 pp. bill, read in parts), or bypasslin an;y way parliamentary procedures, such ils not planned by Pelesi and Reid with the consent of 52 Senators and" fixes" to become effective--ONLY AFTER OBAMA SIGNS THE FRAUDULENT HOUSE BILL! all slgnatures lntended to endorse, retroacively, the changes made by the House . However, those fixes do not appear on the bill when Obama signs, otherwise, the Senate would have ilncluded them il there version for passage, They must appear after Obama signs. Theflixes ecome active after Obma sligns, and thus retrocacively they become a part of the law. Once Obama signs the House bill, it lecomes subject to Senatorial Review, at which time the Senate Changes, bearing the 52slgnaures, become active as "reconciliations." Why is this "rules" procedure dishonest? The changes are not a part of Obama's signed version. He did not lawfully and yet with knowledge of the bill and the impending changes before him (in secret is the corruption of intent), fif slgn the House version into law, absent the changes. The important factor ist he President's signature on the bill, howsoever manipulated through both Houses. This trickery is just anoher version of pork in an conroversial bill that will desroy this nation's economy and enslave the people to the State.

A seat in the Congress is not the same venue as management of a law office. Your Congressional seat is not your personal law office, poltroon. We are not your clients, you arrogant lawyers who intend to radicalize our democracy with some sort of sis-boom-bah Marxist cant of medicalcare crap!

We know how you intend to get Obama care passed---52 SENATORS AGREE TO THE CHANGES ("FIXES)of the House bil after Obama signs it into law, that Senate agreement confirmed by a paper, a letter extrinsic to the actual bill that contains the 52 Senator signatures of retroactive agreement. Lie: the bills of both houses are reconciled by agreement (the fraudulent endorsement paper, ex officio to the bill before it is signed and added only after the bill becoms law. The basic law of conracts is that by mutual agreement of the partiesis lnvolved, one pary exchanges a thing of worth to another for his or its thing of worth, a consideation for a consideration.   Fraud: A slgned bill (Obama)that contanes the thing of worth, the bill as it is slgned is the thing of worth wlith all its provisions, an entity under the law. It, therefore, cannot lawfully add provisions without a reaffirmation by the sgnagtory parties. Afte Obma sgns the addiion by the 52 Senators of the fixes, are added after the bill beoces law. This pernicious way of dealing with unpopulr legislation leaves every proposed statute vulnerable to premptive signatory pillage of adding to the bill outside the signed statute. So it will be in this case, an earmark endored by the sneaky 52 Senators.

A statutory piece of legislation is not a will to which a codicil may be added. The common law contrats of inheritance provides for such changes, but not Statutory law under Conressional consideration and control when once it lis signed into law. Nor can any changes or addions be included as intrinslically part of the original bill without a reconideration of the statute when those autor;izing silgnatures are entered as part of the original bill, ex-post-facto the signing. A Senatorial okay wlithout their fixes is insufficient. To add to a statute, the Congress must present the additions to the people and make their positions known, publically. The Constitution and all other statutes are the people's law for their governance, not the law for the dishonest manipulation by Senators, acting like the Brlitish Parliament of 1775.

Keep in mind that you Leftist zealots are our servants...servants of the people. If that galls you, find another job or go back to your law practice. And good riddance! You are adept at taking an adversarial side, one or the other. You are unsuited by your experience to ascertain, with honesty, probity and discernment, the common-sense aspects of an issue. You are therefore unsuited to lead a great people and a great Republic in a troubled world. We do not want your improvements on the will of the people.

Political skimmer Mme. Pelosi's attempt to empower lawyers in the House (Reid in the Sente) with non-existent power , or to to impose a presently moot law without its formal introduction is illegal and unlawful, will come to light eventually. Her intent is not to urge "Constituional lawyers" to observe propsals in their respective committees but, instead, to propose, suggest amd essentially to promise laws which will override the inherent proedural democratic Constitutional perspectives of relevance, common sense, balance of opinion, proposal of legislation effective by virtue of the lawyers's experence and training. It is not her office to cause a possible law to conform to the wishes of a radical leftist president--to the prejudice of the will of the people, no matter how celestial the law or self-serving is Eva Peron Pelosi. One cannot ethically talk about Obamacare as if it were already the law and needed but brush-up touches i.e. fixes" to reconcile both houses for budget savings! That is a laugh=line when we realize that Obamacare will add 1.3 trillion to the natioal debt. That spin is an immoral deception and it is intellectually dishonest. Such a lie is unethical.

The following are the Constitutionally-authorized venues of power-to-control authorized by the Contitution to the Congress:

Taxes, duties, excizes
defense
regulate commerce
naturalization
coin money
fight counterfeiting
piracies
war and supporting legislation
militia
control of DC
DELEGAE AUTHORITY TO PRESIDENT TO BORROW?
HEALTH CARE FOR HE PEOPLE...? Is that empowerment actully there? No.
not without a Constitutional Amendment!! The people have a right to disobey the Federal Government in this connection. The nation began with acts of disobedience againnst a tyrannical king, Geoge III and his suychophant Parliament, who sw the Colonies as their weapon for Empire power, including the religious, commerciall and voluntary colonies, all.

Obama care is the work of a tyrant--insofar as liberals and leftists worship the incompetent words of Obama, He ought, thereore, to be disobeyed, at our peril perhaps, but demonstrations will convince the "monarch" we do not agree to accept his tyrannical act of specious compassion. . The teaparties are just one deonstration, albeit within the law of peaceable assembly. Pay for care out of pocket, where possible, is another way to show resistance to the polical fraudulent show, the charade of decency and honorable legislaion going on in Washinton. Obmacare is designed to advance the young king's career, not to follow the will of the American people.

I see no specific law that impowers the Congress to demand that the people sign up for, accept Federdal control of, bear the cost and the regulations of., or conform to, threats of imprisonment anf fines, or subject themseles to regulations imposed by the Congress for the mangemen and acceptance of medical care for their pesonal health.

Pelosi and the other leftist liberals who plan to force the people, like British subjects of the king, to bend their knees to the Federal law of Obamacare are asking for trouble from the people. Ameicans are not prepared to abandon their great heritage like cowards in the face of danger. This is especially true when we realize that Pelosi, Reid, and other far left liberals skim money from bills into their personal accounts, like banker bonuses, buy the votes of tweezer Congressmen who want to pinch and sniff at a law, and lobbyists who gamble fortunes to block the will of the people.

What are you running there in Washington, you Poltroons of spending graft and chicanery? You betray the people in your will to follow that European-Iized Fraud in the White House. I think it was C.S. Lewis who decried your sort as "men without chests."

THE CRISIS, by Charles E. Milller, PhD. 12-13-09

POSTSCRIPT: A political tyranny is ilnevitbly marked by the erosion of inividual choice by the citizens in their private lives. In order for the deux ex machina of a tyrant to function well, all the moving parts, the lives of the citizens, must be controlled in the smallest details of their lives. Or else, the machine of the god tyrant tends to break down and become chaotic ,ineffective and painfully transgressive of the lives of the people oppressed by the tyrant. Those connections between perfetly functioning parts and the performanceof the totalty rannhy, in all areas oflife, are evident when minor controls go awry. The people, for example, refuse to use a Federal program, even boycotting it, such as water use by the EPA, Union conformlity demandeded of teachers, and the need for private-sector finance for college ducation show inevitable signs f popular rebellion. The illulsion of the tyrantand his sychophants ils that the parts shoudl adn will work perfectly, whichmeans total obedience to themandates, regulations andfiats ofthecentral government.Any deviation or opposition is punished. Thismakes ofthestate a tyrant, a virtuous monster whodemands total obedience, a had yranny.

Those persons who never experienced democratic freedom for the lindividual may, by chance, never miss what they never knew...liberty. In their ignorance they will assume that the Federal Governmen grants liberty to the individual. God has granted life , liberty and the pursuit of happiness? Oh, come on now! they will retort. Yet there will always remain in literature, in diaries, in spoken communication between generations a residual understanding of liberty no longer attainable, and little comprehended with the life experiences of living generations under a tyrant. The government ilnvented all these things--from the automobilt to aspirin, from the old-fashioned light bulb to organ transplants...?

The process of oppressive totalitarlianism is slow but visible. Mounting job losses are anearlyreinder of the lincompetence of the Federal Government to create a booming economy. The left never surrenders to conservatilve opinion or dicta. It squelche sand fines innovtion, th very sour ce of our exceptional nation. The liberals with their shrewd money management always take over. Inaasmuch as conservative institutions, like the family, the church, the neighborhrood council, small business, seem nnt to matter to the central government, except as tools to be used to icrease centralized control. over people's lives, the illusion of liberty's survival ill remain aong the undiscerning. In addition to job losses, what is another syjpton of malignant opression by the Federal Government become tyranny? Free speech will be shut down...as a free press now b ecome obedient to the outlaw Obama linthe oval office. Has the mainline media ever criticized his sugary appeals for mor emoney, more ;money, a pathetic submission of the press to the tyranny of an historically disconncted black man, his color being the cause for their silence, so skivy are fhey to protec their little souls from the charge of racism.   Damn the truth of Obama's profligacy!

END OF SEPARATION OF POWERS

Citizen.

Minority-leader Mich McConnell's back-up plan in the House (R-Ky) is un-Constitutional. Article I, Section 8 of the Constitution states: "The Congress has the Power...to borrow money on the credit of the U:nited States. "

The Congessman proposes that the Congress delegate that Power to the President of the UnitedSTates, that is, the power to borrow money, in order to raise the debt limit until the end of his term of office, a matter of some 16 months. And that the House set the limit of the borrowed amount at $700,000 , up to 2.4 trillion i three installments, so-called. Madness of an outlaw!.

1. If Obama is re-elected, he will have another 4 years to borrow illegally and unlawfully, against Article i, Section 8, the "end of his t erm" having b en extended four years..

Nowhere in the Arrticle I is the House given evem implicit authority to delegate to the President the power to borrow ,money. .
3. That Power is strictly and Constitutionally the Power of the House of Reprsentatives--"the power of the purse." Article 7 states: "All bills for the raising Revenue shall origginate in the House of Representatives, But the Sente may propose or concur with Amendments as on other bills." The $700,000 in revenuw to be raised cannot be assigned or transferred to the conrollng authorilty of the Executive branch, by law.

4. Such a transfer of borrowing power is unlawful. whether wriltten or transmitted orally, as a delegated power into the hands of the Presdent, Obama, Executive. Nowhere in Article II is the Eresident empowered to accept and to administer such a money-transfer and its accompaning obligations.

5 Nor is the Congress empowered to establish the term for the borrowing nor the amoutnt to be borrowed...details.

5. Furthermore, such a delgatation of borrowing power cannot be sustalined by Congressional fiat, they lacking that authority to create such a law, ex post facto, to begin with.

7. Most pernicious and potentially calamitous for a free Republic is that the precedent of such a delegation by assigment of unlawful athorithy would have for the future. We need only a more aggressilve tyrant to draw authority from the precedent in order to raise this nation's debt to one hunrded trillions of dollars--all our asets thrown into the mix-- if the dictator sees fit to do so.in order to comply with international expectations. We will then have been thoroughly Europeanized. How do you like being a debt=indentured serf instead of a free citizen?

Therefore, the Congressman must either withdraw his back-up plan, for the above reasons, or abdicate his role as a leader and remove himself from office. The American people, when they learn of the mater, will not stand for such a blatant transfer of power, in direct violation of the separation of powers intended by the Founders and strucured and written into the Constiltution. . The urgency behind the Congessman's proposal does not justiify his un-Constitutional back-up proposal.

THE CRISIS, by Charles E. Miller   7-16-11

POSTSCRIPT: We have far too many liberal and letist lawyers in the Congress who, being familiar with the law, are convinced that they are empowered to change the terms and conditions of the written law of the United States Constitution. The old saw "familiarity breeds contempt" applies in their case. Nice guys in expensive silk suits with charming eliquence of speech are too persuasive for the tyros and femce-sitting members of the Congress, both houses. What Miller has skeched above as reasons for denying Congressman McConnell's back-up plan should persuade the unconvinced that any such rearrangement of the Constitutional structure of separation of powers will lead , ultimately, to what the Founders feared most, the concentration of power into the hands of a king or a dictator. The back-up plan is just such a directive to any incipient tyrant who flinds American soil fertile prospects for his empire.

The powers ofthe Three Branches must not be mixed, combined, confused, mutually assimilated in any way, shape, manner or form;...for the protection of the people, the true source of their power...and   for the preservation os America's excepionalist history. . McConnel's plan is the thin edge of the wedge to separate us, as a free people, from our heritage of self=government. We do not need a king or a dictator. His rule begins with the precedent of a unilateral action of President Obama. That precident starts with the proposed surrender to Executive Obama, by Mc Connell, of the House of Representatives's exclusive Constitutional authority to borrow money for the United States. Once that power is transferred, in violaion of the separation of power, it's all over for the United States. We have a confirmed dictator in the Oval Office. The people no longer have any protection from tyranny; we have sold our individual liberties for a fathing and the gifts from our Creator of life, liberty and the pursuit of happiness are forever damned. The State hs become as God, Satan's ambiion at the Creation. Congratulations! Like the Germans in 1933, you allowed

America's desruction to happen before your very eyes, so fascinaed had you become with materialism, secular humanism'a self-auhority and the virtuous State.

TO TOTALLY TRANSFORM IS TO DESTROY

Citizen:

Now that we have a leftist liberal in the White House, we will have a benign totalitarian government. I will call it a regime rather than an administlration, a regime being under the conrol of a single power, in this case, the democratic party, ruled by the "gang of three," Obama, Reid and Pelosi; and controlled by the half-truth that the people are helpless without their babbling opinions of succor and rescue from life's arlarums. This olgarchy of three is their savior.

Gone are the Constitutional constructs of checks and balance of three branches of governent. Our benign rulership conists of the three branches of governmen, dominated by one party, a Europe-oriented Supreme Court that will be drawn into the regime by new appointments, and a press that has promoted Obama, prosecuted Joe the Plumber and Sarah Palin as fantasy-obstacles to Obama's ascencancy to' the throne of power, and declared likeability more persuasive in politics than in character. Obama's radical friends have always been his most meaningful supporters.

Our founders tried to avoid just what has happened, a concentration of powser into the hands of one man (some in 1787 feared that Washington would become a king). The checks and balances have largely been eliminated by the propaganda of a liberal media, by attacks on John :Mc Cain, and by the intimidation of the coal industry, for one, and, of course, Joe and Sarah.

Gone will be the constitutional checks and balances, except by mimicry only. The "gang of three," Obama, Harry Reid and Nancy Pelosi will rule this country. No conservative piece of legislation will pass in the Congress for the next four years, count on it..perhaps, maybe, paper grocery bags instead of plastic.

Gone will be the President's veto of bills from either House, unless they confirm to his liberal leftist agenda. Gone will be the Congressional veto of the Executives orders, treaties and proposals, since they are of the same party.

Gone will be the Supreme Court, now become a Europeanized consensus body and a legislative body, with the appointment of at least one new liberal judge. Gone will be the notion that we are a free society and, instead, "the masses," as socialists conceive of the people--a Eurpean idea of "the people" that mandates an indiscriminate equality enforced by the Federal Government. Gone will be the concept of reward for individual achievement in an atmospere of indvidual lliberty, a n environment of freedom, replaced by intimitdation by an equality of recognition, achievement or not. That Government doctrine and NOT the doctrine of all having been created equal in the likeness of God, all having been endowed by Him with life, lierty and the pursuit of happiuness, will be the doctrine that makes us all equal by Government enforcement. Not the Gospel of Scripture but the Manifestos of the State will govern us despite the visible testimony of he former all around us. And by the way, Senators, if you do not give the balance of your election money to reduce our national debt, you are culpably selfish.

Gone will be the idea of starting and developing a business, since the taxes on managerment and profits will be so exhorbitant as to force the middle-class to surrender to Washington for help, their self-created help having been stripped from them by taxes and regulations. New busines enterprises will be too risky in the face of Federal Intervention, Federal mismangement and Federal intrusion--too risky to venture anew. By this means, a third world nation will evolve that will display a class-warfare engendered by the Marxists in power in Washington, DC.The FederalGovernment will beglin to scorn the rich and fondle the poor, shifting downward the standard or "the rich," and expandilng the definition of " the poor" soas to produce the ideological "aristocrats" and the "proltariat."

Gone will be talk radio, for Obama's revival of the Fairness Doctrine will quash conservative talk-radio and, through boycotts, drive owners to more profitable venues, like Spanish musc, pop music, liberal talk shows and common-man's think-tank shows, and more National Public Radio etc.

In this way--intimidation, oppressive Reichstag measures-- Hitler was able to control the German people. Intead of brown shirted thugs, Obama will use the FCC to silence talk radio as we know it today, and the EPA to intimidate the coal industry, closing the mines and putting hundeds of thousands of coal miners out of work! He is a mad man! No drilling, no nuclear plants, no dirty coal, no drilling for oil in known locations, including shale beds . Or he will blankrupt the industries, not yet clean-swept, with fnes for "greenhouse"emissions. These will be the EPA thugs that will shatter the window panes, not of Berlin's Jewish shops, but of Coal industry plants in a special Krylstalnacht of violence, in the form of troop intimidation. Object and Obama will send in the National Guard to shut them down. Oh, progressive one! Oh, fierce one! Oh, jealous and unrepentant one. Oh glorious Nirvana, utopian America according to Obama.

Don't leave out the church. Mad charismatic replications of buffoon Wrightl's orgy of profanity preaching will evolve, reestablishing Obama's reltionship to his "mother church." Under Hitler, control of the Clergy was mandatory, since most Germans are strong Lutherans. Pastors Freidrich Neimohller, Deitrich Bonhoeffer and others , ultimately hanged for their faith, were exceptions. We should not go so far. But the IRS , another. a third white-shirt thug party (with the EPA and FCC) will be watching the pulpits of America to see that the "groupthink" of the masses is not adulterated by the message of Godliness in government, the righteous political leader, the practicilng devout man of the faith,etc. oblvious to the fact that Christ was not a social but a spiritual reformer. Hitler was seen as a Christian! an early form of Liberation Theology in Germany. He ranted a defense similar to Obama's-- that he espoused Chritianity. Hitler controlled the churches, exchanged the bible, holy chalice and Scripture for a sword, Mein Kamps and the swastika altar cloth. We shoud learnfrom history.

Gone will be America's pride in her military, the most powerful and finest in the world. Obama hates the military, never having picked up an M1. He will reduce our navy...watch...our ready armies...watch...and he will take credit for preventling terrorist attacks on the US, a kudo he has never, ever extended to President Bush.

Obama lives in the world of delusions of power, which which he hopes to execute and to realize under a one-party government. He has hungered for power and is jealous to keep it by his Pesidential edicts. Remember Presidential Orders require no Court or Congressional oversight (Every President, including Reagan,has put out many, hundreds!).

The veto power between the first and second branches of Consitutional government and the nullification power of the Supreme Court will be modified somewhat, but the agency of change by compromise and elimination will turn this nation into a third-world country, known no longer for its brilliance in the sciences, engineering, literature, but under Obama's apologetics, re-assessed for its goodness and likeability before the world. Forget that we Americans have fed, clothed, housed andfought for the rest of the world for one hundred and ifty years. Ignoe the military cemeteries filled with those youths who fought to lierate the world from Hitler, Tojo and Mussolini. Yet, boy-Obama wants us to be liked by our enemies! That is delusional. Only God can change men's hearts, not the government or an Ameican President..

So, do not get caught reading your bible in the classroom or in the newspaper office--or , in time, even on Federal property-- or you will beome in large part a personna non grata. You may even be jailed for a "hate crime," since Scripture calls same-sex unions an "abomination." Deal with it. Now that we have this swaggrstick fraud in office, and who knows or who cares since our grown kids were weaned on revisionist history, rock stars instead of Paul Revere and Winston Churchhill (omited in some school texts), we will somehow make out. The liberals are incapavble of facing dissent. They dodge, excuse themselves, point fingers . The one-party benign totalitarian government will look the same, appear to behave the same, but beneath the workings of the three branches, now welded by the conformation, politcally-correct media, there will emerge the ripe conditions for a more dictatorial authority, one not Christianized by a fool who damns this great and wonderful nation. How can you eradicate over 200 years of history?-- by brainwashing the children to accept lies about its past achievements in government and in society.

Keep your conscience clear, your rifle clean and your way courageous and wise, for we now must face the trauma of one-party despotism. Remember the white-shirted thugs of FCC, EPA and IRS, Bureaucrats all. At Obama's sic-'em!, they will try to spoil your vision in the Krystalnacht of radical social transformation.

THE CRISIS, by Charles E. Miller 11-5-08

POSTSCRIPT: The most egregious transgression of America's istory will be Obama's violation of checks and balaces that initially resulted in the separation of powers. Our Founders foresawt \just such a grotesque , overreaching ambition, just such an attempt to co-mingle the Exeecutive with the Legislative branches and the Judicial with the Legislative, the Executive with the Judicial. And so, the present administration, whch Trotsky would have recognized, is intent upon removing thse checks and balances built linto the Constitutional . Obama wishes to remind us that he is a Constiltutional Lawyer, that he can simply an escuse himself because of that training to co mingle the powers of the three branches of our government. His law trainig makes it lawful to reassign powers...because he knows the law!And that he can do so without challenge, opposition or resistance. Tha is his immaure logic. Being a secular humanist, he needs only logic to esolve theworld's problems.

SOCIALISTS SEIZE TENTH AMENDMENT (X), PEOPLE IRRELEVANT TO POWER

Citizen.

AMENDMENT X:--" The enumeration in the Constitution of certain rights shall not be construed to deny or disparage others retained by the people"

The curious statement in this Amendment X is the RETAINED BY THE PEOPLE -- other rights not enumrated or inferred in the first nine amendments. That clause ndicates that the people hold in their care a power to enact self-protecive rights, in acknowledement of and acceptance of the fact that the Bill of Rights was and is designed to protecgt teh people from ay act of disenfranchisement by the Federal Government.

One of those retained right is the right of a State to progtect itself from physical assault, from invasion, as is occurring in Arizona, the cause of which gave rise the State law 1070. All law-enforcement entities that consider and pursue a retribution by the State of Arizona, under the circumstances of its border assaults, cannot stand idly by and must, and have the right to, protect its citizens with this law, under this Amendment. The right and the power of self-defense, is by this amendment extended both to a political entity, the state, and to the person, a citizen.

If the radicals in our present government can isolate enumerated rights and show cause why they endanger our free society, they need no verbal referene to those "retained" rights, for the radicals in the administration and in Congress will have removed from us the protection of those enumerated rights. Thus liberated thoroughly from the Bill of Rights,the Supreme Court will only appear to administer due-process. Obama once remarked in a comment that that Process is unnecessary. That complete transformation of our judicial system is what Obama and his radicalized Supreme Court intend, with the help of the know-nothings in the media and with the coopeation, surprisingly, of the protestant churches in America. Elimination of religious expression from the public forum has been on the way since the 1960's. Classification of churches as corporations will release an assault on religious freedom by regulatory controls. Regulations have alerady stifled home churches in American communities--but not in China! Any expression of political opinion fromthe pulpit canthreatenthat church's tax exemption status. For its status no longer depends on th absence of profit bu\t on the agency of propaganda, making that church a coroporate entity and therefore poliitical..

Due process if ever it should be abridged by a radical court--as to implement foreign law, Sharia law-- would lead the way to the extinction of enumerated protections, and silence the honor and voice of the people that will no longer be operative to freedom because that voice will have become, to the state, the voice of dead works. The conscience mentioned by Paul in 2nd Corinthians and in ancient Hebrews of the New Testament (cf: Strong's Concordance) would fail to be of any value in courts of law, as discerning argument to defend an enumerated Right. The effectiveness and efficiency of the Nazi SS was achieved by men without a conscience, moral discernment having been destroyed by State brainwashing--Hitler's intention e,g, to raise a generation without a conscience..

A moral conscience and a political right are indissoluably linked. For that reason, nowadays, the state is beginning to assume the mantle of virtue, thieving this token of righteousness from the extant protestant and Catholic churches (by conrol of abortions, proclamations of liberty from the pulpit) and the Synagugues of America. Once the State becomes virtuous and is so recognized by the people, there will be no ober dictum, no higher authority to challenge and to assail the supremacy of the State, for it will have seized that status and station from God Almighty. Mark me. I know how men's minds work. Therefore, the " conscience of the state|" will do away with such dead works as religious freedom, freedom of speech, freedom of assembly (association) and the other enumerated rights in the Bill of Rights. Once the enumrated rights are expunged, the retained rights come next, including the right to own property. The Kelo case has set he precedent.

Due process to defend the citizen from what...? The very concept of due process then becomes meaningless. With its loss will come the extinction of privileges and immunties that protect the citizen from the Federal Governmentm the basic purpose of the Bill of Rights and the separation of powers vbuilt linto the Constitution. All these protections are linked together, so that when one of those rights enumerated in Amentdment II is extinguished by a liberal court ruling, the total protection of the Bill of Rights is on the way to extinction, Right by Right, privileged by privilege, immuniy by immunity. Thank God the Court in its recent decision retained the right of gun owners to keep their guns! This, of course, was a defeat for the Obama gang of pirates. Only a people desperately igorant of or intimidated by big government or destroyed by their own self-will to illiteracy...illiteracy affects 20 % of todays adult population... are vulnerable to the loss of their Creator- endowed rights. Inroads into freedom of religion will be preceded by inroads into freedom of speech in the name of feelings, self-eseem, equality of judgement, relativism of opinion and a politically-correct anarchy of social control by speech control. You might have to assemble in your bathrooms to discuss politics, as happened in Hitler's Europe. Perhaps even today.

Ti invite tyranny in government, remove rights one by one, those enumerated in the Bill of Rights. and then, logically--explained to the dumbed-down people as "dangerous" to their illiterate society-- those enumerated rights, once they are gone, will make of those "retained" an illusion that is easily expunged by a liberal feel-good court ruling , based on German, French, Spanish, Dutch laws. This destruction of our Constitutional protections for the citizen, will be deemed--that word again-- to have been held by a people who cling to their religiona and their guns. Such debasing ingratitude will appear despicable and unspeakably ugly to those who love liberty.

Obama and the socialists will point out that they gave due process a chance and it failed to protect. Many Americans will be disenfranchised becaue of their political opinions. The State will now assume the role of protector that replaces the people's once enumerated Rights. The "democratic" sloganeering will go something like this: "Vote for your protectorate in Washington. They are dependable, they are responsible leaders. "

"Candidate" will become a banned word. See voting poll Oversight Manager to fill out your ballot . (As in some unions, no secret ballots.) The Czar will help you to select the right leader. Have confidence. You did not want to learn English or to finish your education. In your face, iliterates! The entire voting process will be regulated and controlled for efficiency and by permission of the office of voters held by that Czar appointed by Barack Obama or his lapdog successor. You won't have a clue as to what you have lost...unless your grandfather tells you. Except for the remnants of a brilliant, productive and free sociiety once called "America", you might as well live in Europe. There everthing is already set up for you...Obama, Pelosi, Reid, Rahm, Axelrod et al. One problem: you wont't have is the luxury of the remnants of natural rightsover there. There will be no hospitals in Europe, Michelle, to give you half a million dollars for your name and no fantasy flights to New York to see a play or to Africa to connct with your forebearers. . Of course, there is always the Coeur de Elegance of Paris for your fashions.

THE CRISIS, by Charles E Miller 6-29-10

POSTSCIPT: The liberals and leftists are clever at re-defining the English language, changing certain words to accommodate their Marxist ideology. Those "rights" left to the people (Am X) will become not rights, subject to definition, but feelings, capable of beinshared in a virtuous State...one big, happy human family! The virtue of the State is; not the righteousness alluded to in Romans 13. The viltue promoted by wizards of the law, money-elected officials, virtuous members of the Federal oligarchy, is the virtgue of circumstance. That virtue was once callibrated to be called situational ethics, changeable as the situation changed so that a robbery could be construed by a corrupt court as a gift, a murder not as a pathological homnicide but as a compassionate end-of-life deliverance...as Obamacare's death panel nowt threatens, a part of political tyranny. Other changes in the language will disgrace the pious believers of the Christian church as homophobic destroyers of the new-age State of total forgiveness. For after all, the test of virtue is the grace of deliverance; the virtuous State will be able to deliver all criminals as victims, a process now starting with the release of 46,000 felons into general society because they are too costly to keep in overcrowded prisons. Forgive them, like the fobildden Jesus Christ! How slowly Obama's declared "total trasformation" cotinues, before the eyes of the general public...who should not be alarmed because the State has deemed them also to be virtuous, members of the virtuous State. We,by these transgressions and culpable changes have lost our soul, our moral beginnings, our perspective on the meaning and the value of life, on religious conviction and faith in Almighty God. We are losing our way. A religious revival maybe the only power that will ave this great nation awash in the swale of ingratitude.

MARSXISM DESTRYS CONSUMER BASE

Citizen.

Debate on the Senate Healhcare crapola begins November 30th. It will prove as close to insanty as a non-clinical charge can be when 100 Senators at least sixty of whom, voting straight Democrat, will vote to pass their piece of Politicalcare. It bears only the superficial appearance of being careing for th health of Americans. No having read the bill a this point, how woul they know? I have heard conservaive commentator Kevin James read portions of it. Its thrust is not to advance care for the health of Amricns. Its thrust is to advance and secure the jobs of the Poiticians and bureucrats in this Administration. It will please many of them to feel the edge, the weight and the control of power in their hands for the first time in ther lives. To hell with the people. There is money at stake here!

Obamacre is caring for the careers of the Democrats, the tight-fisted liberals in the Administration and the lobbyists and special interests who are today in the process of buying votes for the bill. One-seventh of the American economy is for sale.

Healhcare rationing will be the lesser evil if the Senate bill passes. Core of the collapse of this nation's economhy will be the crushing of the (wealthy!) middle class by taxes. An ilncome of $60,000 for a family of 4 is "wealth," five grand a month with over a quarter in rent, payments for the car, schooling costs of the kids. food prices going up... You are out of your bloody minds, you fools in the liberal Congress and the incompetent Admilnisration.

When small shops and businesses can no longer afford the insurance foisted on them by the Obama nightmare in Washingon, DC, they will have to shut down.

Having shut down because of the inability to pay for employee insurance, stsores and shops will be forces to lay off workers. This will destroyt the consumer base of our economy.

Ours is a consumer-based economy, not a labor-controlled society. America's propserity comes from her people making things for profit beynd coats of labor and mhinery.

Without money to spend e.g. prosperilty, the people will be unable to buy goods and services. , The unemployed will run out of unemployment entitlement Insurance and the government will not be able to extend it wilhout funding from profit. That ils the "shovl ready" economy Obma promises as "jobs creation.". Literally millions will be out on the sidewalks of America, physically impoverished and hungry, the governmen broke, the consumer base literally destroyed by the liberals and massive appearane of bigger and bigger government-generated poverty . Hunger will emerge. The long soup lines of the 30's will be nothing compared to the rampage for food and medical care. But hospitals, deprived of loathsome profit-making, will have to close their doors.

The liberal fools in the Congress do not comprehend the connections in a system of supply and demand that turns on the word, despicable to Marxilsts, earned "profit.". Health needs will become of less desperation than will mere survival. The impetus of present prosperty will have run out when the government, deluded by Socialista into believing it can CREATE JOBS, fails to do so and must borrow from other countries to survive.

As fot he elderly, they are not cost-effecive. Let them die of natual causes. Note the accent on the Utility value of the individual, no longer a person created in the image of God.. but a digit like a slave field-hand, valued only for his ability to pick cotton to swell the master's income...and so designated by this adminisration. UTILITARIANISM IS REPLACING HUMANITARIANISM. So much for your proud, ilneffective and fail-ready health care, Elitists in Washington!

How did this whole debacle begin? It began with that Marxist incompetent bowing-and-scraping fraud in the White House, consumed by the deception that (1) proflit is wrong and evil, (2) the rich idle. middle class have gotten too much money (Marxism) and must be stripped of profits, wealth, capacity to purchase, that is, to acquire loathsome property.

Increasling taxation is the inevitable result of the improvised Federal taxes to pay for the monstrosity of healthcare for every livng soul, infants, pre-teenagers, aged--he useless eaters, and especially the lords in the Democrat Congres who are too blind to forsee what would happpen with their overburden of taxs dumped upon the job-makers, the "wealthy" middle class. Those taxes are destroying our comsumer by enforcing layoffs. the jobless without money to purchase goods and services. Unless we can reverse the destruction of our consumer-base real soon, I predict we will reach a 25% unemployment rate by 2020. Credilt will lsustailn an e conomy only util reasonableterms forepayment c annot be met.

You are by the blindness of your ignorance and lack of common sense are in the very act of detroying the peoples' producive capaciy to buybecause they will no longer be employed for profit to the employer..

You delude yourseles and scratch your backs to think you create jobs, you bureaucrats. The jobs that are opened to paper pushers are opened by the use of tax money, not the use of profit based on consumer demand. The former will last until more taxes are added or withdrawn. The latter will survive when goods and services gain increasing appeal to sonsumers so as to result in increased production and therefore in a labor-surplus i.e. profit.   Scornful of free-market profit, You fill bureaucrat vacancies. The taxpayers, not consumer-based spending, enables you to meet your Federal payroll.

THE GOVERNMEN DOES NOT CREATE JOBS IT FILLS VACANCIES. THE GOVERNMENT PRODUCES THE JOBLESS AND BORROWS TO MAKE UP LOSSES IN ITS REVENUE.

THE ENTREPREENUR MIDDLE- CLASS PRODUCES THE JOBS.. REPEAT: THE ENTREPRENEUR MIDDLE -CLASS PRODUCES THE JOBS. DON'T FLATTER YOURSELF, NARCISSIS OBAMA. GOVERNMENT SIMPLY CREATES WASTEFUL VACANCIES, CREATED NOT BY MARKET-PROFIT NEEDS BUT BY MANDATE TO MEET A TYRANNOUS POLITICAL WILL. YOU WILL TRY TO MAKE MARKET-PROFIT MEANINGLESS TO AMERICANS. YOU BELIEVE THAT YOUR PERSONAL POLITICAL WILL "ENCENTIVIZES." LIKE ALL TYRANTS, YOU ARE A NARCISSIST.

America's,middle -class economic complexity is the result of capitialist free-choce eterprise for profit, Pesident Obama. (As a Hawaiian Islander, you did not grow up in a dynamic competitive environment. It shows.)

When you tax the middle-class shops and stores to "spread the wealth" for your insane, single-pay procedures and insurance program, to the extent that shops and stores have to lay off employees, you create poverty because you destroy the consumer base. LIberals and leftilsts have lived in their bubble for so long they have lost touch with reality and with the people, who elected them..

Idealogue obama not comprehend the connection between the consumer-capacity to purchase and a business capaciy to remain in business in order to supply a consuming public. He makes the former impossible through exborbitamt taxes. The latter will become impossible without purchasing power, earned money...as compared to entitlements.

Present-day healthcare rests on this axiom: high taxes plus Federal over-regulation lead to layoffs and to inferior goods and services, which layoffs and inferior products equal consumer unwillingness and inability to pay for such inferior goods and serfvices. They can no longer afford to consume what you produce. The upshot of this axiom is more layoffs until finally, you immoral and impractical Johns in the liberal Congess will have destroyed our consumer-based economy. Having made us to grovel at the feet of crooks in Washington, you Meia can, bowing deeply as to the Emperor, kiss Obama's image in public with impunity. For, after all, it is not the people but the obsequeous little Chaplinesque dictator you would please. for one reason only, he is black. You are indentured to him out of fear.

THE CRISIS, by Charles E. Miller

POSTSCRIPT: In 1776, we destroyed your level of tyrnnny with guns when the English Parliament and King George III would not listen to the people. The more

Americans you throw into jail because of their objction to the overburden of taxes (read: fines), the cosllier will it become to keep them imprisoned. And the costlier it will become in wasted years and lives.

There is missing in all this power-abusing morass of incompetence not just the abuse of power and the incompehension of our leaders to appreciate the fruits of a free economy. There is in the mix an element of revenge by the liberals to impose measures of retribution against the people who voted for them, a form of payback by Obama and his crooks in the Administration that includes his 39 Czars and his infinite number of EO's, Execuive Orders. Judicial Watch has filed a FIOA request to check out the former leftist activitis and connctions in order to determine their anti-Amerianism.

By demonizing Bush, Sarah Palin and others to the politicalright of center--an ilmprovised politial paradigm---, you expose your impotent rage. You libral democrats reveal your incapability to think creaitvely. For you are the frustrated prisoners of an ideology that captivates your minds and holds you in the bondage of its drab, worn-out and tried, inquisitoial and faceless theology of State control and power as the path to utopia. I vewnture that most if not all of you do not know what a "utopia" is and therefore do not know when you have arrived--which is now, today, in America. Ask a refugee from Cuba, Venezuela, Soviet Russia, Nazi Germany....

1) Marx writes of "labor's surplus" as the profits that result after deductomg the cost of labor per se. He represents this excess as "accumulaterd " rather than "earned." wealth. He ignores, disreagards or is ignoirant of the advantages to labor of management's reinventment of that surplus. Marx features profits as an accumulation for persosnal autocratic gain, as of a company employer and not to be shared with the workers, his employees' o r inthe hiring of more employees or in expanding his company or in introducing new products-- the reality This misconception of the purposes for profits constitutes the delusion of Marxism's closed ideology of class exploitation.

Some, of course, goes to employees as a reward for risk-taking and imaginative enterprise. Marx did not, however, believe in those qualities of management. He scorned reinvestment as a waste of labor's surplus "earnings." He saw that ecess as an illeglitimate contribution of the proletariat to the wealth of the bourgoisiem of a class-society in eternal struggle.

2) Marx leaves out of his equation,7marketplace supply and demand which are, in a free-to-act market-demand requires reinvestment to meet increased consummer demand. Marx is fixated not on a dymanic market of change but on a fixed market of labor surplus for the selfish benefit of management. Obama is fixed in that trap of thinki8ng that rules out supply and demand marketing. The trap presumes a statguc consumer base in total dilsregard for s ocietal growth and shiftling product ultility and demand. Whethger these last two facors elighter lincrease or decrease is none of Marx's concern, since his condemned CEO presmably has secreted the company or corporation rofits in a corpooration jet or a yacht. .. We can now understand Marx mischaracteri\zation of management and, logically, Obama's

shared disrust and distortion of management...particularly corporate CEO;s.   Obama hlas not evlen a rludimntary understanding of a dynamic company's use of profits because the very word is a curse to his life, as it was ot his mother's life, even though she profitted in the banking industry. Barack's Martxilst ideology blinds him to reality. It is with the results of that blindness that a free society must deal. He will not allow options to Marxismto exilst...if he can help it. While he swquanders our wealth, he pleads causal innocence, thus his detached manner of address before the people.

THE CRISIS, by .Charles E. Miller, 11-23-09

POSTSCRILPT; When Barack Obama promised thtsoon the FEderal Governmentwould have thousands ofshovel ready jobs REAready for the unemployed, he tipped his hand as a Marxist. A shovel job ils a job of labor only, without aproduct to how for the work. That meant to Obama that Federal jobs would pay for the labor of their job offerings at a day's wages. That mans, u;der Marxilsm, that "labor surplus" that is, capitol raised in addition to the labor0 wage--the seductsive profit--is usually seized by management toinvest iln personal luxurie,s like corporate jets. The lMarxilst theory leaves out the relinvestmentof that surplus, that is moneyafter payment sof operatilng costs and lab or, Obama believes,geilng a Mrxist, Tjat s urplus is money earned by th sweat of labor and elongs to them, or to the Eeral government, certailnly not to management orto investors. Crashmanagement and the ilnvesnestors, show them what honest possession reallyis,take over the car companies.

Marxists do not accept the reality that labor surplus, or capital, has an honest use in a consumer sociey. The avowed Marxist blives that once the laborer, the orker, earns his wage, he then is working for the profit of his employer which, let us say, ils the last two hours of hisworking day. In six hour she has earned his wage. The last twohours are for his employer;s profilt, and that iswrong. The Marxist is convinced that that wage surplus is seized greedily by management and the inevestors, to augment their own money in terms of dividends. Worker surplus is holy, earned by proletariat labor, the fruit of which is stolen by the bourgeousie, CEO jet and car company owners. This is Obama's creed. He felt perfectly justified lincrashing the GM stockholders meetilng and replacing the Manager wilth a Obama drone.

Marxists do not accept the reality of supply and demand. In a free market, every lay-off is one less consumer of one or more consumed products because of a lack of earned income. The Marxist governmemnt, which we currentlhy have, possesses a shovel-readyljob mentality, that is, payment of labor for its efforts and wlithout the profit taken y a parasitic employer. The shovel-ready mentality does not consider the markeplace value of the product, lin the case of trench diggers, a trench. But what about a thing produced b y the "shovelers?" Greedy CEO's inlate the price, not just to cover labor as an operating cost . They inflate the price for their greedy seizure, and for the investors. Obama thinks that is unfair and inequitable. Demand results in an increased price for a product, the excess from the sales which surplus become capitol , ils used to hire more employees and to furnish present employees with a wage that enables them to paricipat more widely in a consumer market, to buy what they need and want. Obama does not accept the connection between increased labor surplus...profit...and markert growth in jobs , new products, inventions, risks. He is an economic illiterate and remains so even when shown the connections between supply and demand. Deamand encourages the use of capital to incrase supply. If the demnd comes from a foreign coutry, Obama sees the use of profilts from that demand as evil, motivated by greedy capitalists, the investors in the foregn maket. Capital and capitalists are evil parasites on a society which the Government must control...as an act of compassin through regulation.

Shovel-ready jobs do not produce products, but only supply a living wage for the unskilled labor, hopefully. A society identfied by its masses of shovel-ready jobs is what Obama wants, a utopina society where every worker earns a living wage and there is no labor-surplus, no profits, no capitol. That is the bottom line. Taxes are the Marxist means to suck profits and thereby capital from the economy. That is occurring this very day. Job-growth dies. Obama, a deceiver, hides behind a pretended empathy with the people, of whom he is contemptuous.

Do away with reinvestment capital, profits, the "surplus" fcreated by labor above and eynd the level of a fair wage and you will have a third world agragian 18th century rural society once again. Businesses will close, industries shut dowsn, products disappear, inventions cease. because there is no profit to stimulate competition to produce a saleable product of value beyond lits labor cost to produce. Labor becomes requred only for the most basic manual jobs, roads, more roads--get the M:arxist promise? A consumer-oriented society feeds off of labor...it is predatory... according to Marxists, therefore that labor-produced surplus, known as r profits, must be dispersed and taken out of the hands of management and put into the hands of the the Federal Government through taxes. The Feds can do a more efflicien job, whatever ithe product or service consists of!. That is the delusion of the Marxists and of Obama. He would control consumption by Excutive fiat and appointed bureaucrats who, by the way, are paid by the shovel-ready labor... that remains, when the economy collapses. That M:arxist extinction of profit wil nver work in America because the Federal Government is an incompetent replacement for private, individual intrepreneurship. There are just too man;y produce-manufacture decisions that have to be micro-managed by intrepreneurs!

POLITTICAL APPOINTEES TO SUPREME COURT

Ciltizen.

When Barack Obama appointed Elena Kagan and Sonia Sotomayor to the United States Supree Court bench, political moves by President Obama to advance his career and his ideology at work, he appeared to have overuled discretion in the selection of justicess to preserve America's will . Yet his choices reflected his policies in their statements.that featured the US Constitution as a "living, breathing document," subject,therefore, to being changed on the face of it to accommodate the circumstances of the case. . Absurd! Both women augurerd liberal decisions based not upon the literal meaning of the document's words, not upon precxident and not judgementsthat would prove good useful and conscionable for this coury, A "living" Constitution mandated an   interpretation that would give sanction to their personal opinions about social justice, that ils, invented law--as it is rigtly called--or, as it has become known ...legislation from the Bench.

The pollticization of justice in America will mean the end to our brilliantly designed judicial system. We will become increasingly like Europe where, especiallyin France, a person charged with acrime must prove his   or her innocence...and where there are no courts of appeal, Appellate Courts. In America, leaders even more anbitious than Obama will appoint judges who will represent not the law but the liberl policies of the party, the Democrat arty in power. The President will pick justices who mirror his policies in their decisions. In the lower courts, judges will be elected on the basis of their party politics. Public employee unions will attempt to "manage" these choices and the elections per se. The jury system, hallmark of our trial courts, will fade away as irrelevant. Evidence to justify a cause of action will, increasingly, be manufactured as opinion, as in Europe. In due time, a citizen will be considered, guilty before trial, at which time the odds if a hydgenebt if ubbicebce will be stacked against him or her.   All of this corruption of our judicial system will issue from the injection of politics and the self-serving pressures of politicians who wish to manufacture law viz a viz court decisions based on their living, breathing feeligs and their notions of equality and fairness. The Kelo case is one such"change. Another political decision will be the relase of 46,ooo convicted felons innocent of "serious" crimes, by order of the supreme Court. The Dredd Scott case in the antibellum South, presided over by by Judge Taney, was an earlye example of a political decision trumpting the law, a slave was property instead of a free citizen under the Consttitution.   Jim Crow laws ere political. A judge whose selecton represents a President's poltical amblition and his career is a poliical appointee rather than a Constitutonal appointee!

THE CRISIS, by Charles E. Miller   7-10-11

POSTSCRIPT: The hidden deception in describing the Constitution as a "living Document" is that the law as it is written , its meanings clear, becomes an instrument for expedient rulings. An expedient ruling by the US Supreme Court is one that neither coflicts with current Administrative policies or damages such preconceptions as "fairness," "all are equal,""racism," concepts of "groupthink" spawnd by the :Marxist-socialist ildeology. The basic law of the land, the Constitution, therefore, becomes amenable to popular judgement, poitical dynamics of the party in power, and the personal predelections of liberals and leftists in our government. In short, the Constitution no longer is or remains the fundamental law for the three branches of government. Indeed, they become indistinguishable, the Supreme Court making laws that become acts of legislative meaning. The Congress spews out thousands of mandates that have the force and effect of judicial rulings, that is, cannot be challenged and if disobeyed are punitive. Furthermoroe, the Executive takes upon himself the powers of the Legislature, the Congress, in order to create offices outside the scope of his Constitutional autority. And so there it is, the "living Constlitution" no longer useful as law but as groupthink guidance, popular advice and consent, the opinions of judgfes iln black robes, an undependable protection for both the people with their Bill of Rights and the officeholders, who can no longer depend on the written law to defilne the limits of their authority and the leglitimacy of their legislative actions.

Never mind. The Constitution is alive; that's all that matters. Just be sure to feed it liberal greens. Blind men! Liberty will become anarchy, freedom will become illusory, America is will becoming an illusory Utopia. No sweat, no struggle, no risk or loss, no pain, no victory or defeat or competition or failure. Are you stupid common people happy with yur elitist rulers? You should be. Brace up! Our big-government outlaws say you should be happy. Just a little more time. Marxist Obama's Utopia is on the other side of that hill. He knows better than our Founders what you need. Have you confessed your needs to President Obama's politburo of 14 scions, appointed parilahs of knowledge--law, medicilne, business--who have all the answers? They impatiently await your response. Call this number: MEphisto 666-666-6666   You will gladly share 80% of your income with them the demons i.e hard workers. They understand your pain. Their sweettalk will separate you from your gold and your independence, you will be the happier for the gifts; take their word for it. They will share your sacrifice. and your transient sense of loss...only a sense, mind you because the actual gold was theirs to begin with. They have their newly-printed paper dollars to prove it. Don't forget that you reside on their property, their eminent domain, vulnerable to the next ambitious developer for The People's mall.   Selah.

THE STATE AS GOD

Citizen.

I derive many of following concepts from Rousas Rushdoony's book "Christianity and the State." Consider this letter a book review of Dr. Rushdoony's very excellent and enlightening exposition of the hostility of God toward the un-righehteous State. My contribution is the appliation of his concepts. Romans 13 predicates a righteous State, God's agent and minister, that operates within God's will, the which evil-doers should fear when they fail to "subject" themselves to the righteous State, that is, to obey the laws of their society. That was the State envisioned by America's Founders. Their vision was not a thleocracy but a secular State whose leaders respected the law, honored God and practiced honest dealings with the people. Our leaders today envision a secular, globalist God-expunging State that excludes the faith of our forefahers, eliminated God from schols, public forums and State recognition while at thesame time, they admit satanist worship as legitimate relgious worship in the military s ervice and delete the name Jesus: from the ministries of all chaplains. A Federal judge inTexas has recntly ordred that the word;s;"God" and "Jesus Crist" be deletd from memorialand graveside services at the National VA Cemetery.

Barak Obama's "completely transformed" State---from liberty to oppression, from individualism to masses conformty, from enterprise to submission, from opportunity to Statist regulations, from productivity to entitlement--all these tyrannical features were contemplated by Marxist. Radical Obama is currently hoping to acquire total power, disguised as relativistic compromise with our history and our laws, a dictatorship of the Presidency. To this end, he , Pelosi and Reid have arrogated sovereignty unto themselves, finding it expedient to trick the people into acceptance of Obamacare without a legitiate House vote of the Senate bill for Obamacare. The vote was for a "reconciliation" of the Senate bill the Senate bill being "deemed" , or raher presumed," to have passed...WITHOUT A HAND -COUNT OF HOUSE VOTES FOR THE SENATE BILL. To "deem" a bill as having passed is a substitute for an actual vote on a bill the text of which must remain unchanged and identical when passed between the two Houses. To "deem" is not to vote. To deem is to presume agreement and that is fraud of a major piece of legislation. Passage was, therefore, outside the purview of the US Constitution. The; House rule of presumptin is not intended for such a monumental piece of legislation! It is or dinarily reserved for attached pieces of legisltive funding of the main bill.

But by using this device, which changes one-sixth of the US economy, the Congress usurps, abuses, oversteps the power of the Constitution, which has total sovereignty to determine and to control the course of this nation of laws. The Constitution! radicals scream...what a ploy to avoid reality Reaity? Americans have yet to experience the destructive costs of the deemed-to-have-passed Obamacare bill. To suggest God's role in our government sounds irrelevant to the pragmatic matter of Constitutional passage of the legislation.

I am not silent as to the ultmate consequences but I say, at this time, that such a device of trickery--the House can make its own rules--augers the destruction of a nation by default.

We will all suffer in that destruction, which will result from the " transformtion" by the piratical seizure buried in the White House scheme. What else can you call boarding the car industry and with sabre flashing, tearing contractual laws apart? All three boarding pirates of the Regime were involved in the fraudulent deemed "passage" of the Obamacare bill. They were in fact, the conspirators of a despicable fraud against the people.

Do you see any humility in their magisterial words to control the people by fraud and precedural manipulation? Small wonder Obama demeaned "process." Obmacare was "passed" by a deception of the people Be aware that when the State by example, choice and ignorance eliminates God's providence from its customs, values, laws and traditions, it becomes the source not just of all power but of counterfeit ethical andmoral virtue. The State has then empowered itself to enforce conformity and uniformity in the cause of ethical "fairness.". The virtuous State ,without any other reference than itself, can then deterine the kind, extent and expression of its own power. The State ean do no wrong. That is Washinton's attitude today. Those given un-Constitutional powers, a the 39 Czars and the cabal of stooges for Obama will autocratically and alone, judge what is and is not "fair." Because it is absoluely virtuous, the State will determine what is criminal, wrong, unjust and illegal and thus the government in DC, will establish its closed system of humanistic values at which man is the center. The State is then. by its own self-declaration qualified by judicial consent to try war criminals as civilian lawbreakers with its perfect justice. There is no higher power. The State becomes the source of virtue. Churches, religion, home training are all irrelevant and must be allowed to atrophy in the New Age of globalist America.

Dishonesty is virtuous when the means justfy the end. Freeing prison inmates is virtous if the act will balance the budget. Taking from one man, his home, his business to give to another citizen--by eminent domain without domanic values--is virtuous if that other "needy" person lacks a home, a business, a hard-working income. This transfer of wealth is called an entitlement by the radical present Admlinistration. The seilzure of private property to give to another private person becomes a virtuous act in the eyes of the virtuous State. It is virtuous politically to brainwash kids in the grades by White House videos because those kids will later become productive socialist citizens as a result of having been brainwashed to produce for Uncle Sam. Self-ilnerest ils the hallmark of greed.

It is virtuous to destroy the notion that the banking , the saving of captal is wise, prudent, advangtageous, and risky, because capitalism is the anathema of fairness in a democracy where all must be equal. It is virtuous to control medical doctors but not trial lawyers, because the benefits to the former are rooted in greed but the trial lawyers practice a degree of fairness in their causes of action that benefits all of society. Whereas a surgery may be botched--the fear behind lack of tort reform in Oamacare--a trial for equity brings rewards to the deprived. That is "fainess" in action. A the sole souce of virtue, the State, can therefore do no wrong.

As its powers increases, the State's zeal to punish dissent increases. We see that today, wherein a Senator will attempt to cut off dissent by punishsment in one form or another. We see that today in the cowardly silence of the media to expose Washington retributon against dissent. Penalties can consist of jail, fines, illicit (expedient) taxes, disdainful laugher by the President, mockery of the people and denegration of the nation's history. These are all devices of the tyrannical State. It is morally wrong to replace the courts and legislatures with violence and open revolution. It is expeditious to see the benevolent Rulers focused on expanding government power in order to control the people's lives and, according to Marx, spread the unjustly-acquired wealth not just to Amerilcans but to the resj of the "suffering" world. They, the people, will become the slaves and footstools to this process of change. Propaganda! Already, the mainline media are literally the propaganda arm of the Obama administration.

Barack Obama is attempting to create a class-society of controllable workers for and under the heel of the government as receivers of the government's largesse. I am convinced that he intends to crush the wealthy and middle-class into one, undefineable mass of entitlement recipients, docile before the new god of the State, and happy and contented to receive the provisions of a central government that is evil in its intent and pratices. I'm waiting for a Minister of Information, a Goebbels of propaganda, to emerge and be named an Information (Propaganda) Czar. Is it already the Press Secretary?

By making their authority absolute, the Rulers become an abomintion in God's eyes. They usurp the will of a righeous people, in complete contradistinction to Romans 13, that promises a righteous government and an obedient people who need not fear the State unless they do evil. Without God the State is the determiner of the extentm the nature and manifestations of its power. According to Romans 13, the State is the minister of God. When, however, the State presumes to be our material and, implicitly, our spiritual savior, it transgresses God's law and becomes evil. Salvation from what? From needs, from the injustice of wealth-seekers, and from the unfairness inherent in our history. When, in effect, the State becoms the total provider of our human needs, it takes over God's role in human intercourse and practices evil; (God! Ask God for food stamps!) The government becomes evil when the State promotes its salvic power, salvation from evil, salvation from death, salvation from immoral acts...as defined not by Scripture but by the corrupt will of the Marxist State and the rulings of a manipulted Supreme Court. Gone will be conscionable acts by the government and by the people. Gone will be true justice but rather. in its place, the advent of a mediocre society in education, medicine, business and local administration. Gone will be the competiion that elevates an exposes supriority in work, product and ambition.

At this point the State replaces the church, replaces religious faith and establishes itself as the arbiter of morality, virtue and justice and without God the inventor of laws to suit its own will. That is anarchy. A man has the right to the fruits of his own labor? No, the State has that rght--Obama's State--and, seizing those fruits, he will redistribute them according to its doctrine of "fairness." That is Europe's godless, mediocre and unproductive environment.

The State, i.e. government is God's agency for the welfare not of the Rulers but of the people. Thus Obama's agenda is for the welfare of the Rulers--leftists, trial lawyers, union supporters, lobbyists. enjoyers of taxpayer bailout emoluments--and not for the welfare of the people. The Government, i.e the State is today a Godless entity. We can, therefore, expect it to lie to us, to cheat on the people, to innovate laws that break the Constitution, to seize powers delegated to the other branches, to indebt the people for four gerations and by trickery and obfuscation eventually wipe out the Bill of Rights thereby, purging personal freedoms in the bill of Rights, while ultimately destroying our great country. The cowardly silence of the "free press" is a Federal indulgence. The media no longer has a soul. They are a ridiculous joke. "Truth, what is truth?" the media ask, like Pontius Pilate at Christ's trial. Truth is what Barack Obama says it is. N'est pas?

Man was not created in the image of the State but in the image of God. Therefore Barack Hussein Obama is first answerable to God. As the State, the usuper dies--that despite all signs to the contrary--man's responsibility for his actions and his freedom will increase. For there comes the death of freedom whenever man becames god. The modern humanistic State is a jealous god and will tolerate no contending rivals. Indeed, it indulges in immorality (see lies, scandals, back-room deals, bribed votes in Congress) and tolerates no moral declarations, actions or presumptioms of independence and individualism among the people under its control. In fact license given to imoral acts, such as plunderinging of the txpayers, by the State's subtle, unspoken sanctions, engenders a fear from which the State promises protection. Thus we will witness the growing tolerance for immoral conduct among the citizens as a means of Statist fear-control through tolerance.

Accompanying that tolerance for immorality among the populace comes an increase in taxes to control human behavior--ac companied bya lessening of true self-government alongside ever-increasilng power. When a State becomes prophetic of the future, it assumes the role of Jesus Christ and the church. As the State becomes more powerful, it increases its pressures to conform and to become uniform...in today's language--to be fair. It is politically-correct to endorse a mindless "fairness," but nobody knows exacly what it means! To give awards to people who have not earned them? To make sure that no family has to make a sacrifice greater than anotherin or to have a successfu marriage, to acquire an education...? Fools! Obama's attempt to "transform" America into a Utopian nation of enforced equality will bring this nation crashing down economicaly. We are not all equal, Charlatans.

Note: that with the increase in power comes less true government (benevolent abstention, cautious intervention, careing regulation) and more taxes. We are in that broiler today. Obamacare is not governmen at its best. It is Statist compulsion through taxes to benefit the bureaucrats and leftists in the administration and in the Congress. They never saw somuch money! The goals of the authoritarian State are control, regulation, jurisdiction and

82

power. The control is established in order to authorize the Rulers to manipulate the economy and all institutions that contribute to that economuy. With that control comes the power to invent new laws, break the basic Constitutional law, judge the citizens without charges and usurp power from existing branches of government....by making them indistinguishable.

Obama legislates, Obama silences the court and invents (legislates) Czars with (autocratic) powers not granted to them by the Constitution. He is, in effect, an outlaw in charge of the government, smirking at and mocking the people who put him there. He is a fraud, an incompetent, a radical manipulator, a ne'er-do-well from chicago's machine politics. He promotes disharmony in order to justify invented-law changes in government. His 34 Czars bathe in invented powers over the people. Talk about legislating from the bench! Barack Obama legislates from the oval office!

When the State becomes a terror to good men, it has ceased to merit obedience. (Rushdoony) l repeat. When the State becomes a terror to good men, it has ceased to merit obedience. Remember that. And when under these circumstances religion is merely tolerated, it is not free. It is allowed to exist by fiat, condesension, tolerance of the all-powerful State. It is therefore subject to removal, cancellation and condemnationby the State. As the salvationist State becomes the agency of providence, it replaces God. When the State can do no wrong, the citizen's freedom is illusory. Under these circu;msances of the inculpability of the State, the citizen has no right to differ with the State, that is, to differ by any attempt to oppose a provision that has been secrely embedded in Obamacare, as the Biodata card. It bears repeating that when the State acts to replace God in the minds of the people, it becomes the providential replacement for God to control the actions and especially the thoughts and speech of the people. In short, resistance is made to appear unfair, unlawful, and anti-social--the croaking of the Leftists--because individual thought as a matter of dissent is contrary to the "wisdom" of the State. All resistance is, therefore, hostile to the omnipotent socialist State, regardless of what the Conservative-traditonalist resists. Dissent is made ot appear seditious! In order to insure "fairness", there appear the pressures for conformity, compliance and uniformity. At that point, responsible expressions of honesty in Rulers of the all -powerful State are no longer God's command but becomes a human utility, an expedient act, a politial-correctness Adoration of the State and its Rulers becomes politically-correct in all venues of public life, including the pulpit.

Therefore bald-faced lies are permitted. even encouraged in order to advance and to enlarge the State because lies are useful to the promotion of ever greater power-control of the people. Again, the end justifies the means. By ruling out God in public discourse, by attaching fines to expressions of faith in public throught, by trivial court rulings, by punishing Christians, the State asserts its humanistic, absolute power. In order to legitimize Obama's lies as truth, the State is compelled to consider the common people as stupid and ungrateful and, as a shibboletlh of Marxism , they, Amerians, are the illiterate (European) " unwashed masses."

Our ignoramus-of-history President is a consummate liar. His words and his actions are not to be trusted. hs ils an outlaw. It follows then that to legitimize his lies about his agenda, he literally must in his absolute authority--by his actions--transgressive of God, consider the people as incapable of caring for themselves. Therefore, he urges us, the people, to thank him as god--a whimper he has expressed in his most recent dishonest judgement. I say again, that he is not to be trusted in either his words or his actions. Having grown up in Hollywood, I am innoculated against his smiley, smooth-talking sort of movie-star charisma. I honestly believe that my highschool educaion in the 1940's excels his collegiate training at Harvard!. I learned the value of character and the meaning of truth-search . I learned to think.

He has learned none of these. Karl Marx, Alinsky and his leftist piratical crew do the thinking for him. Leftist Idealogue Obama offers opinions as searching thought to the people. Cheers!

THE CRISIS, by Charles E Miller

POSTSCRIPT: Brack Obaa is a nrcissist,theeasure ofhisself=love going sofar as to attemptto destroy anentire nation,its people andtheir wayof life hw believes, withoutviolence. He expects thereby to ake of himself a messianic figure of a glorious silent revoluton in America,begun almost solely by himself. The scope of this monstrous ego cannot be measured, but it can be seen as he again and agai transgresses Constiltutional laws, puts the nation in economic and military jeopardy and makes of our forefathers renegades who would not have commprehend the majesty of his vsision for a utopina America. He underestimaes the ingeunity,the courage and the enterprise of the American people. This generation will live to flaunt his policies of Federal largesse.

OBAMA'S ABUSES OF POWER

Citizen. "

This letter deals with President Obama's ongoing abuse of power:
1 . Bargaining with the enemy is treason. Apologizing to the world to demean Amercans' pride in their country then sealing the destructive and demoralizing perjoratives by handing out to the world taxpayer dollars as tribute money to the third world.

2. Secret political deals with Iraq not to withdraw until he succeeds to office for credit. Behind doors, dishonesty Exclusion of some of the unfavorable media from press conferencs. Withholding the truth of old-croney payoffs.

3 . Purchase of power by hidden bribes to leftist Congressmen and Congres women. Pay offs to and Bribery of Unions, campaign supporers, leading to the corrupt suppostion that the taxpayers are the poor and incompetent drones to meet Obama's wanton agreements, in contradistinction to the will of the pople, who are made to appear as the servants of govenment. Thus, he has distributed taxpayer monies freely to cronies like ACORN and Leftist organizations. He has mollified the jealousy of the world with our money and our labor.

4. Lying to the people to achieve outlaw ends e.g. his Ideological agenda. Obama's entire two years have been loaded with subterfuge, lies, broken promises, corrupt tactics to fool the people. He speaKs of civility yet practices abuse .of Bush, the Supreme Court, the CEO's of GM, Chrysler, etc.

5. Payoffs to poltical suporters--banks, insurance companies, Wall Street CEO's.

6. Intimidation tactics. to silence the media Seizure of private property--car companies.

7. Legalizing Federally-mandated transfer of property from one private citizen to another upon threat of heavy fine. A "fine" is not a tax, a play upon words to legalize the deceptive violation of the Costitution, allegedly under the commerce clause. What a joke! A play upon words to deceive the public. A fine is not and cannot be a tax when it is a violation of a established law. A tax is, generally, for all citizens under legal criteria. .

8. Tolerance of invaders--open borders, America's sovereignty destroyed, Bush was a paticipant in this ruse, continued by Obama to enlarge the democratic vote.

9. Overtaxartion to spread the wealth. Enforce risky loans...housing debacle resulted.

10. Outawing guns, first, then ownership-deprivation (by seizure) of people 's fundamental right of self protection. A disarmed people invites attck.

11. Enforcement; of privte contracts--as health insurance, surrender of privagtet property to another idividual by the deception of eminent domain

12. Repeated violations of US Consitution that override the will of the people and undermine their confidence in their government. He does this by his expansion of meaning of the "commerce clause" and other Constitutional restraints on the Federal government. Example: His Executive right to select officers for the performance of his policies led to the installation of some 30 unapproved of Czars, whose duties and programs, even now, are unknon both to the people and to the members of Comngress.

13. Control the private decisions of individuals, such as of diets, lights, cars education, penalizing non-conformers. The DC control of childen by seilzure of parents' rights in making dcisions about education, diet, currilcula....This particular control is the foundation of tyranny, is and always will be--control the next generation, if not by fiat then by intimidation.

14. Fostering growh of alien religion in America...Muslim

15. Emdorsing security measues that divide Americans. Ev evntually, a number on our foreheads, or arms, as in WW II Fascist oncentration camps.

16, Packing the Supreme; Court with idealogues who believe in a "living ie changing Constitution that meets socialist-state expedient needs

17. Endorsing the concept that victims are the brutalizers and the attackers are somehow victims of society, etc. This devisive concept leads to the class society of the right and the poor, a Marzxist concept of the bourgous and the protletariat.

18 Brainwashing children in the grades to believe that they are servants of the state, to detach and alienate them from parental influence and control

19 . Forging an outlook that proclaims the guilty to be guiltless viz a viz a corupt Attorney General acquitting the Black Panther intimidation of voters.

20. Execution at will and with ideological direction of presidential fiats that have the force of law, usually hidden consequences or brazen Marxist outcomes. These are approved of by a one party Congress...
wheneverthey are made known, which is probably seldom.

21. Denial of the validlity of our Repulican democracy's historicity and the value of a two party system, an olugarchy beilng the result, e.g. Obama, Reid, Pelosi.

22 Obvious disdain for the will of the American people

23. Willful subjection of generations to come by his extravagant spending, a playboy adolescent with the authority of a king and the intelligence of a criminal (a crafty thief of our way of life) and the perception of a single-minded Marxist demagogue.

24. Hiding behind his fixation on a former president as the source of his troubles.

There are more abuses of power not listed here. Any President guilty, yes, guilty of such "indiscretions" is not fit to be President of this great and powerful and exceptional nation. The man must either be forced to resign or impeached by the House and tried by the Senate, all the evidence made visible to the American people and to the watching world. The facts are out there. The cost cannot equal the 1.3 trilllion dollar budget or the projected 14 trillion debt in the future and the corrupt ownership, through loans , by an enemy nation, communist China.

THE CRISIS, by Charles E. Miller   12-21-10/ 1-13-11

POSTSCRIPT: President Obama's repeated violations of the US Constitution makes him unfit to be the President of these United States. And yet, intalled into office by the will of the people, he has made of himself a tyrant over their lives, in large part by casting them intounemployment and insurmountable debts of trillions of dollars. Losses of jobs and people's homes havecompounded their misery and, in many instances, their desperate efforts to survive...all because of Barack Obama's polities and his draconian attacks on privagte industry, personal income and a free economy. As a Marxist, it has become increasingly obvious that he hates capitalism. Because of his violence against contracts and CEO positions, and his renegade attacks on the car industry, he could accurately be descried as an outlaw.

Obama nherited his Muslim faith as well as his angst against class power, whatever its source. He hides his Marxism behind a position of silence sof neutrality while in the Congress. His early associations with Mrxist Saul Alinsky are well known. What he broght to the Presidency was neither experience nor resolve to do the will of the American people. He brought, instead, a desire to diminish a great country in the eyes of the world and to treat the will of the people with a cavalier disregard.

This was his way of demonstratilg his independence from America's exceptionalism and its hsistory of personal liberties, creatlive ahievements in science and industry, and free trade. His outlawry springs from an anarcissistic-self will that brooks little or no opposition; he, therefore, must always be surrounde with those who agree with him. He has absoslutely no comprhension of the American zest for competition as a means to achievement and fulfillment. Thus his outlawry is the produce of self-alienation, concealed behind a gift in spoken English, aided and abletted by his teleprompter. His self-alienation finds expression in his many trips to the golf course, his junkets abroad,his love for crowds, his projction into almost three dozen Czars.

Why should this self-0alienation be of any concern in the performance of his duties as President? Just this: it is not a self-imposed aloneness but, rather, a rejection of our society, its fundamental law and our way of life. His abuses of power are an expression of self-alienation from the American people because they represent, not freedom and accord but, instead, they are like moguls and aristocrats of old who lived to amass wealth forselfish purposes e.g. CEO's wlith corporate jets. He is the righteous one. One should never forget that, as the explanation of mamny of his actions...that he is the righteous and the appointed one, by Allah. His alienation is best expressed in hissquanderlust. and iln his unconsciona ble acts sof outlawsry, the breaking of promises, of the Constitution, of the faith of the American people.   , to our great detri;ent and the snhacklement offture generations.

CIVIL TRIAL FOR JIHADIST WAR CRIMINALS

Citizen.

The shootng at Camp Hood was commtted by a Jihadist Muslim as an act (1) of obedience to Allalh's command to kill the infidels, and (2) as a response to military separation of radical :Muslims from "infidel" GI's.

One well-known columnist has stated in his column that liberals regard the multiple murders and woundings as (1) the result of medicalization, and therefore (2) the Sheik is a "victim" of "medicalization," ie. drugs.

Lacking to this concept are (1) perpetrators and (2) motives. Perpetrators can be the pressures of a profession and the patient-to-patient confidences shared with the Major at Walter Reed Hospital and in camp.

A profession can influence a man to such an extent that his words generate feelings of retribution. But other "victims" of ilnfluence shed similar experieces as returningf veterans, therefore that thesis does is not valid or ethical.

Patient confessions can generate resentful, even violent feelings, but self-discipline should control any impulse to violence. This is especially true in the light of other clinical workers sharing the same experience with vets.

Now we reach the ultimate conclusion, that if the perpetrators of a crime against a "victim" in this case the Major, it can be inferred tht the self-conemnation of the Major was a part of the post-stress syndrome ("medicaliztion"), and therefore patient confessors ("returning stressed vets") cannot be accused of harboring a desire to murder the "victim" or cause him to murder others. Thus, the only powerful violence-generated factor was Sharia Law .

That law is apparently embraced by the "victim" Army Major. That, I think, is the discernable truth of this case. The causal factor(s) are not post-traumatic stress and/or that he "broke down" or he was a treatable "nut case."   (effects of his "medicaliztion") These politically-correct, erroneous judgements are held by by liberals media, the Time Magazne and the NY Times. The Major was never deployed.

Those quasi-medical judgements mislead from the truth. They lack the wisdom of truth that is silenced in order to defend the judges from charges of anti-Muslim religious bias. Such moral cowardice can possibly result in a hands-off treatment of the murderer. He will be temporarily exonerated from the mudrer of 13 innocent soldiers and wounding of 31 other Camp Hood soldielrs, in order to give him medical treatment. That compassion is unrealistic, politically correct, evasive, maudlin in its sentimental feelings, cowardly and an endangerent to the safety of others under the same ruberic of "innocent by way of insanlity, a word readily exploited for political purposes." No "Twinkies" this time.

Count on it: in another case, the Muslim five Gitmo detainees soon to be tried in a NY Federal Court will plead innocent for lack of witnesses (3,000 dead witness from the grave), and innocent for for lack of (battlefield) evidence. A conviction in acivilian trial requires motive and evidence/ The Gitmo combattants stand to be freed. A conviction in a military trial requiress situational evidence without a motive or hard battlefield elcvidence. They would not be freed.

Declared innocent by the cilvilian court, they will then sue the people for false imprisonnment--to be treated as US citizens innocent until proved guilty (4th Amend). Their Defense will stress--"deprived of life, liberty, or property without due process of law" under (V), and each man will complain of being forced to "witness against himself." and under (VI)--point to the 8-year lack of a "the right to a "speedy and public trial". under (VIII) -- meantime, sufferilng "cruel and unusual punishment, All of these Constitutional protections for the Amercan citizen can be entered as arguments to free the accused Jihadists, having been given "due process of law."

THE CRISIS, by Charles E. Miller

POSTSCRIPT: This situation and trial will reverberate internationally as an example of America's evil system of injustice and ilntenatinal judidicial outlawry. Of course, our protections against self-inicrimination and presumptive innocence before proven guilt are left out of the accusation. The intent of those liberals who wanted to place the Gitmo detainees in an American civilian court has one explation: they wanted to invalidate the due process claise of our system of justice by its finding the detainees innocent of murder... for a lack of evildence! The same leftist critics of our system of justice,even now, intend to internationalize our protections for the innocent and to declare them invalid if the accused is not first cleared and accepted for trial in a csze by case review in the United Nations or the Hague. :obera; Kistoce Lemmedu has expresed his willinness t look at outher judicial systems in order to be better infomed about ours.

The justice systemof sthis country is unique in the world of western societies. Forfilve reasons:
(1) A person accused of a crilme is guilty before he is proven innocent lin France.
(2) No other societies a jury system such as ours.

(3) Evidence must first be screened y a judge before it is admitted into the trilal, and then earsay is also made to be evidence.

(4) In certain societies either no witnesses are allowed to testsify or, if they are permitted, they must qualify as relatives of the accused

(5) A trilal in Framce is heard before a judge, and without swearing to prevent perjury. These are a numberf of the differences. One must remember the impact of the Bill ofRilghts on courtgroom testimony. Justice Kenney has saild that he would b e willingto see a Muslm case tried under Sharia lawm a 7th century code of urisprudencetha totally lacks the compassion and rigfhteousnesss of our system of justice.

STREAMLINING, AN EXCUSE TO VOID LAW,
OR MAKING CONRESS IRRELEVANT

Citizen.

Rino Republican (Tenn) Lamar Alexander and propagandist Chuck Schumer (D-NY) of the growng "apparatus" currently plan to "streamline" that is, short-cut, the democratic process of Congressional oversight of executive staffing by limiting the 1,400 candidates for Federal functioary jobs to 1.000. Colleges have their reduction of admission numbers; that isn't the point. Congress is not squeezed for space or stressed by applicants' ovrhead.

These two manipulators attach the cause that higher numbers of candidates for supervisory, management, and control positions in operations of the Federal government are too many to review and decide upon to fill the slots available. Tht objectionabrly higher number bottlenecks staffing, making staff appointmens too slow and difficult. Gracious!

Such a "streamlining" (1) makes Congressional oversight irrelevantt as the voice of the people; and (2) Sreamlining discards, ie. makes irrelevant, the Consitution's separation of powers and its function of checks and balances of power. What we see in Obama's adminisration is the gradual destruction of those protective walls--strucures with purpose.

Obama, viz a viz Alexander and Schumer, would incrementally concentrate power by eliminating oversight, as he has done with the Czars and his Executive Orders, now in the hundreds. He thereby makes the separation of powers as checks and balances irrelevant to his purposes. There is no check eilther to theczars or his Pesidential orders. These acts are conceiled and executedi secrecy.

Not Executive selection but selection without oversight is another step in the process of eliminating Constitutional control that protect individual liberties, taking the power of the people out of their hands by making an oversight function of the Congress. irrelevant. (Czars, Excutive Orders, Functionaries)

He is certain to load up staff possitions with his radical Chicago pals (ACORN) leftists, liberals and all Democrats, making his one-party system the --streamlined--model for fuure elections. In due time even the Congress, although visible, can be made irrelevant.

The key word for this manipulation of protective Congressional oversight is "IRRELEVANT." When Congress becomes irrelevan and their power is dimished to facilitate speedy, expedient access to power by a dictator, his powe perhaps, we are flinished as a free nation.   Power shifts from the Congress ,the voice of the people, to the Executive, the voice of one man.

Obama is his own authority. That is anarchy. He has found rapport with the dictators of the world in his station as President. He finds our friends irrelevan for his agenda vision of One World. He is and will continue to be an outlaw, politically incompetent and utterly selfish toward the American people. His speeches are strings of finnessed propaganda lies.

Staff appointments without the people's ovesight ratchet up his lust for total power. He does not care a fig for this country, its history, its culture, its liberties, its God of the Scripture, and its people except that   he can use them to gain career power.

In another two years, we could have a fascade shadow government, conceived in secret, directed out of sight, hidden from the people, ruthless in its marxist agenda to destroy us, and immoral to the point of evil. Obama's voice is Godless .

His vision is one-world government, achieved by the exercise of his narcissilstic, messianic mind-set. with the help of his liberal-media disciples and the 40% who still believe he is apostolic. His sympahizer Americans are not necesarily evil; they are alll around us.
Yet they are pathetically ignorant. (Our schools teach UN one-world-ism, not American history.) Many of them, who cannot be bothered to vote, don't really care about this nation's future as a Contitutional Republic. For them, America's past is...irrelevant. The Constitution is irrelevant!

THE CRISIS, by Charles E. Miller 4-17-11 4-19-11

POSTSCRIPT: Elected politicians who reject the will of the people when they consider staff positions empowered by law relegaties the authority represented by the voters--the will of the people: What is that--party policies? The politicians may call it "sreamlining." This elision in democratic empowerment is, infact, the eradictionof the people's authority, an act of cotrolled radical--pure--anachy disociation from the people. Obama's one-world govrnmentwil mandatges the removal of all Constitutional safeguards of the people against the Government. His maxist vision will leave no room for the traditional statutory safeguards in the form of Amendments, or the basi 3- Branch Articles of our Constitution. They will become empty of meaning and impotent for action. They will become irrelevant under Statist regime.

FREE SPEECH V VOTER REFORM

Citizen

Let me remind you, perhaps a majority born since the 1960's who felt that the study of American history was not worth your valuable time. From my forthcoming novel rmrnfrrf on the Amerlcan Revolution, "Our Struggle," I quote Sam Adams, firebrand of the revolution and nephew to John. He has called a meeting of the Sons of Liberty in the Old North Church basement. Sam's express purpose is to fire up the rebels to do something about the TeaTax recently layed on the Colonists to bail out the bankrupt East India Tea Company. Sound familiar? They will dress as Indians, board three merchant ships,that lie at Boston harbor docks. They will dump the crates of tea into the harbor...a song was written celebratilg the Englishman's enormous cup of tea.

Our revolution had much to do with taxation without representation, the king, in his royal folly presmied the Colonists would obey his onerous taxes, one after the other. Samuel Adams is speaking:remind you, however, that three of the King's own war-ships stand just off the wharf, mid-channel, and they will be watching our every action through their bloody spyglasses. "Count on that, good men...those blighters will not dare to fire on us lest they damage thr tea crates. The King would not take kindly to such bad manners." Laughter here and there in the hall. "I have some more detail, gentlemen of the forecastle." Laughter punctuated the reference. "We take upon ourselves this mission because...well...in protest agalinst the Parliament's bloody marketing in which we...colonists of the Crown...tea drinkers ourselves and common citzens of the Realm, We are and continue to be denied a voice in the entire matter. All too often those consummate periwigs of gold gild and Temple-fashioned wisdom have left us out of their accounting, except to tax us to hell without a single sigh of representative appeal, consent or objection. "

The hall burst forth with loud noise and whistles and more foot stompng. Adams was loathe to end the response. "Are we to continue to allow that accursed Parliament to outsmart us for our labor, our sweat, our money by taxing the life from us whilest we sit over here like grave markers and are not permitted a peep of speech? Must we continue to a endure Parliament's bloody taxes for the remaliner of our lives without a representatlive to voice our will? We are British citizens also!"

The clamor grew in volume "Why not then rebel?Why not then Rebel?"
"Why not now?" came the angry voice of Greagory Toteman.; The hall exploded

into raucous, angry calls, hoots, applause, foot- stomping and other signs of agreement, many also standing in the group to applaud and with their hats in hand, waved Adams on. "TheTownsend Act...remember that? Contributions to the wealth of London's merchants...rescinded, they say, and the damned Stamp Act heretofore and only God knows what will come next are the acts of bunch of saclliwags, high-toned, wigged and silk-suited, noble gentry of the realm who look down their noses at us as sif we lacked the common sense of ordinary beggars. They have once again denied us a voice in a matter that affects all of us, and we are quit of lheir shinanigans...are we not?" Exceedingly loud shouts filled the meeting room.

You want to know what happened next. Read my book and find out. They took action, and action is still not beyond Americans when they are aroused and the mission is both honorable and necessary for the life of our democracy. Would that the liberals and their cohorts in the coming election learn from our history. There are things initiated by our government that we will fight for....and fight against..with our blood if need be. Gold has corrupted our Congress; that is a major cause for its being broken. Bribery of the votes of thle people by Congressional promises.

Gold has corrupted the Free speech that is at the heart of our Democracy. Gold has corrupted the politics of our elections, lobbyists and corporations who control the people for their profits. McCain says he will remove pork from major leglislation, but he allows gold to prohibit free speech right up to the Primaries (30 day rubicon) and for General election (60-day rubicon). Who do you think you are, Senators, to tell me I cannot defend unborn life right up to election day? Are you the sons of hell. If I did not have a better opinion of you, that's where I would tell you to go separate gold from speech, Senator and allow the people with a cause, who a e members in an identifiable entity like a pro-life group, to voice their opinion without the sinister and corrupting gesture of gold to salt the message. Remove gold from the McCain- Feingold bill and let the people speak rlght up until the final hour, Senator. The McCain-Feingold bill smacks of tyranny. So lbe it, if you refuse.; but you can remove the fangs of resistance if you will simply admit that "Political communication" (the FCC stamp)can be and must be tolerated within the 30 and 60 day limits established by the Bill...when money is removed from the pleading.To the devil with the FCC! I didn't elect them.

It is the money that corrupts the communication and that imposes a phoney time-line on free speech. It is the money that is the disease of enforced silence. It is the money that mandates silence in violation of the First Amendment to our Constitution. the money that abridges free speech, not the politics of the communication. And it is the money, the soft money, that constitutes a bribe. If Senator McCain wants to be consistent and remove pork from important legislation, he should remove the brlbe money that mutes our free speech of political communication. Then I will believe his intentions

So long as the money is not separated from the political communication, even if coming from a well-known entity alike Right to Life or Universal Health Care...the organizaztion assumes none other than a persuasive message when it does not come bundled, wrapped and conditioned by that entity's war chest or tts members' open purse. That separation cannot be done? Then democracy has become a purchased commmodlity, a whore in searchl of moneybags. Free speech at the last minute in a general election, Senator McCain, without the soft money, is the American way.To remove that impediment in the McCain-Feingold bill is to remove the gag from the mouths of millions of Americans who do not have a lot of money but wish to represent a viable and legitimate cause without the interference of Washington bureaucrats.; Your hard-nosed position on Voter Reform may cost you the Presldency, Senator. Any other way could spell revisionism for this ation. Do I make myself understood?

THE CRISES by Charles E. Miller

POSTSCRIPT: The Mc Cain-Fengold bill is itended to block heavy funding of legislatin at the last minute, thus to sway the results of losing legislation with gold. The signal flaw in the bill is the silencing of political communication at the same time. It need not have been so. The voting public ought to be allowed to voice their convictions, feelins and opinions right up to the election deadline without a dime to support their views. You can be sure that oppostunists will exploit the silence to their corrup advantage with any communicationt that passes for sensible cliff-hanger bias.

CAP AND TRADE POISON

Citizen.

The waxman-Markey Cap andTRade bill nowbeforeCongress will utterlydestroyAmerica's fee market economy by imposing production caps to reduce carbonemissions. Thats the dirtylittle secfret of these two swilneherders. whoi think f themselves as representatives of the people. The represent theend of America wlith a bill that will degrade and destroy industry asmuchas Obamacare willdstroy medilcine iln America.

1)Nine lines of reason disprove the validity and workability of the CARBON CAP bill byWaxman-Markey The bill was passed out of sight-- without reading or debate and is therefore dangerous, perhaps unlawful and certainly destrructive of the economy.

2) The bill attempts to shape and therefore control consumer demand by enforcing levels production. This artificial tyranny will destroy the production industries, farms and family money management.

3) To control demands the Federal.goverment try to control supply by imposing artifiical standards on engines of production, farm machinery,factory machinery and home usages and demands for food,clothing, heating oil.

4) This artificial control is tyranny disguised as envron;mental improvement. Waxmanand Harkey presu;mes that the American people are stupid suckers for this machievellian scheme.

5) With the enforced reduction in demands for products and services to offset any increase in carbon emissions, there will come a loss of jobs the likes of which we have never seen This econstructing of the nation's economy is nothing less than the expunging of capitalist system, free-choice investsments in a goods and service to help others and loss of honest profits.

6)That system has made this nation great. The Cap and Trade will reduce America to a third world natioin, outwardly unchanged, but inreasingly hollow economy that finds itself u;nable tos upply the needs ot its citizens..and of the rest of the world. Free trade based n supply and demand will become obsole in favor of central socialist control of the means of production in order to control carbon

emissions, but emission s are not mentioned, nor are the connections between the production of wealth and polutuion defilned. b y the EPA

7) The bill shows Obama to be a liar--he will not raise taxes on the middle-income Americans. He lies about transparency in his administration, shown now to be a corrupt powerpac power manipulators and tax dodgerss, thieves of tax money and conspirators tocheat the people out of their substance. Scam thieves in fine suits! The bill shows Obama; to have charmed the press and media who do not crltique his bill--being kmno-nothings--passive, enhralled aspirants to power >and tools of a growing Fascist central government. The plan is to convenrt America (worthy of Jeremy Wright's hatred) into a one -party nation--Fascist-Democrat. In another twenty years, third- world illegals and legal migrants will think:America finally got it rilght. Wrong.We had it right before that charlatan Obama and his corrupt henchmen and henchwomen took office. Enjoy your cheap sandwlch, your counterfeit shoes, inoperative cars and the lack of the former good life,which you have thrown away. The stench of your corruption in the adminstrationr reaches all the way out here to California,which has its own corruption. The immoral sand unethical stench is >the death of freedom in America, just the beginning for that charismatic demon in the white house. >He breaks promises, lies his way to acceptance to agullible people, and condemns this once great nation to the misery of third world socialist-fascist poverty of means and sustenance. ;

8) The effects of the bill;s regulations bill will have no impact on the climate. The bill will not create (or ADD new) jobs but will destroy them. VOTE NO ON THE WAXMAN-MARKEY CAP AND TAX BILL. and will do nothing for the environment. It will destroy capitalism in America.

THE CRISIS, by Charles E.Miller

POSTSCRIPT: Should this billbe enacted into law, there willbe requlired tens ofthousands ofCarbon Police and aystem offines. Thje bll will kill thriving industries, putting their emplyees out of work. The governmentwill require the instllation ofarbon meters ilnhomes and inindustries and meter checkers to monitor thecarbonolutput fromthese two sources. Changes lin machineryd esign wil cost industries billions of dollars, never tobe recovered insales totheir consumers. GThousands of industrieal bankrupcies willbe the consequence ofthis "renovation." Cap and Trade wil result in product loss from the world's most inventive andenterpising nation, America. The EPA will become a government within a government. Extorion and bribery to skirt the law will abound, the corrupting of America. Product desgn in certain industries , such as paint, and uuto manufaure, will cheapen to allow those industries to conform to the new carbon laws. "Quality products" will disappear from the nation's production lists. The income from affected ilndustries, now lessened, can no longer support other industries they considered subsidies, tangential, dependent makers of this or that product. If furuew " environmental scentists should prove t he falssity ofthe premice of carbin as causal, the investments by industries affected would be irrecoverable. America would slip intoa pre-industrial age of primitive machinery and low production. Trade wilh foreign countries would skyrocket as a result. As with oil now, dependency on other countries would reuslt; Ameria within decades would rot, decay industrially and slip into the shadows of a third-world nation.

PRESIDENT OBAMA, TRUTH DODGER

Citizen

Barack Hussein Obama failed to conmnect the pieces of evidence in the Dutch to America Delta flight 253, therefore, I find him guilty of negligenc in the performance of his responsiblities as President who is responsile for the security of this nation, and dereict in his performance as Commander and Chief of the armed forces. In both commands he has broken allegiance to his oath of office. The failure to connect the pieces of evidence is his failure, based on nothing more than a failure to brief CIA Chief Leon Panetta, his show of contempt for such non-golfing details, his lack of a normal person's curiosity, and his inept manner of getting at the CIA's "latest evidence of terorism directed against this nation." Barack Obama cannot fob this error off on any other member of his cabinet. He must face the charge of negligence in the performance of his duties as Commander and Chief, and as as protector of the Constitution and of the people whom he serves. .

He cannaot ignore what was evident to the world, yet he has attempted to avoid direct responsibility for the lapse in security for the Delta flight from Amsterdam. CIA chief Leon Panetta is equally responsible for his lapse in observation and/or for his failue to communicate the evidenc to the President. Head of the Department of Homeland Security Janet Napolitano cannot truthfully claim that her security apparatus "works." It obviously failed in his case.

Barack Obama conceals his negligence by a pretended innocence of knowledge as the reason for the breech in security. CIA chief Panetta was his choice for chief of that agency. If they did not communicate, that is the fault of Barack Obama and Panetta alike. If the evidence, the killler's father's revelation of his son's radical jihadist bent, the one-way fare, paid in cash, no luggage, the Yemen's name--all p pieced togther constitutd the suspicious "unconnected" pieces of evidence, where was the the responsilble anti-terrorist action. Those pieces were all evident to Panetta. He, too, voided his oath of office by his failure (1) to act on the evidence and (2)to communicate with his Chief.

Why did Obama ignore all hints sof trouble and pretend to be an onlooker, taken by surprise? He does not want to offend the world bankers of the Bilderberg Group, the Council on Foreign Relations, the Trilateral Commission all of whom--the world's bankers and political manipulators-- see Obama as their New World Order puppet (and we "the people," as their slaves). Barack; Obama did not want to apper to be politicaly incorrect, thus his deception. He seeks to be the leader in "Global Justice." He would have us view the terrorist as a lonely young man disenchanted by his father's wealth. We are supposed to believe Obama's plea to bring to justice all those involved. Such ils lthe state of global interconnection nowadays that passes for diplomagtic relations but s, instead, politically correct bull crap!

The terrorist's intention was evidence by his failure to ignite the explosive. Obama pretends surprise. He pretends dissociation from the CIA evidence. He pretends to tell the truth to the American people. He lis a deceiver, a keystone-cop actor, a promoter of fake "transparency" n government.

President Barack Obama does not champion the best interests of the American people, except to exploit them like any politician, but he champions "World Justice" of a "New World Order " (superior to our Constitutional justice) controlled by the milti-billionaires of the Bilderberg Group, and their operatives in the Trilateral Commission. He pretends to champion the people. Wall Street was bailed out. What happened to over nine trillion dollars looted from the U.S. treasury in the process? A cap on Excutive salaries was a fraud to appease the gathering suspicions of the American people. Whereiln the Constitution is that power giventon him?

Pretense is the name of Obama's socialist game. His campaign promises of transparency, 5-days to read a bill, etc. were rhetorical trilcks, devices, the skewing of language. World bankers are using him, gradually making the Congress ceremonial (their Health Care vote) as they increase their puppet's power viz a iz the office of the President. Wait until Obama's "civilian military force just as powerful, just as strong, just as well funded as the militlary" gets under way--a national police acivatedby the BIODATA card for all citizens-- and FEMA's construction of Camps for political Dissnters becomes apparent . You will see the induction of youths 14-28 into service brigades, (a mere 3 months) the Jungensbund of Fascist Germany come alive again. They will be brainwashed to detest our history and to hate historical America, accused of race-hatred and imperialism. There is aleady afoot in some middle schools the plan to start American hisory at the Civil War Reconstruction! The SPP (Security and Prosperity union with Canada and Mexico) is not dead, just dormant for a time.

The man is evil. Barack Obama is an ugly ingrate who trashed conract law at GM, who trashed dozens of dealerships which in some instances were the life-work of the entrepreneurs, he has shown his contempt for the "profit motive" many times--though he is a billionaire hypocrite--he knows not the struggles of the middle-income American, he is a danger too the future of America. The dumbed-down main-stream media continue to worship him like a god. He ignores Blacks, he crams his adminisrtation with crooks and nepotists and power-mongers, he lies again and again to the people, he breaks campagn promises, scorns transparency by secret deals, he ignores the truth, he fawns upon our enemies, chastens our friends, plays games with race, feigns a beautific innocence by his manner, brings lobbyists and moneyed supporters into his regime, dismisses God as irrelevant and would make the people servants of the State, starting at the second grade with an"obey me" video for the kids. .

        In a word, Presildent Barack Obama is a fraud as a leader of the greatest society of Western Civilization, the target for radical Muslim jihadists, whom he would cozy up to. He has abused his power office so many times that he stands as a rebuke to our founding Fathers. He has created over 40 czars, czars to whom are imputed significant discretionalry powers neither stated, implied nor tangential in Article II of the US Constitution. They are Czar bureaucrats who are not answerable to a Congress elected by the people.

        Artiucle II, Section 2 in referrence to the Executive powers, reads in part: "He shall have the Power by and with the advice and consent of the Senate to make Treaties..." (SPP, NAFTA. Copenhaggen?) "...provided two-thirds of the Senators present concur..." (see the vacationing empty chamber) "...and he shall NOMINATE, and by and with the advice and consent of the Senate, shall APPOINT Ambassadors, other PUBLIC MINISTERS and Consuls, Judges of the supreme Court,and other Officers of the United States, whose Appointmns are not herein otherwise provided for and which shall be established by Law, but THE CONGRESS may by Law vest the Appointment of such inferior Offiers as they think proper in the President alone, in the Courts of Law, or in the Heads of Departments."

        NOTE: the reference to Power in Article II, Section 2 is always back to THE CONGRESS, not to a singular kingship power possessed by the President. A one-party Congress may reduce the opposition but not eliminate the direction of the flow or transfer of that authority, or eliminate the constraints put upon that power. We have a Presiden who in his benign arrogance ignores the direction and the source of that authority. He preempts powers that by law belong to the Congress and, in effect, awaits their conciliatory affirmtion without proposal and concurrence. This overreaching of presidential power leads to a ceremonial ("rubber stamp") Congress who, like the British Parliatment of king George III, agrees without disagreement to the king's proposals. I resent and rebuke the Presiden for that overreaching abuse of Executive power. I, too, am a citizen of the Republic.

        The President has the Power to appoint officers to carry out his and the Congress' assignmens, not the power to impute to those officers (Czars) that they are totally at liberty to mandate their own non-statutory agency powers--without oversight, without a suckered-in mainstream media opposition. For example, as the FCC becomes more and more powerful and far-reaching, the Amendment I free speech right of Americans becomes increasingy threatened, minimized and manipulated as unimportantprimarily to the government and less so to the people. Thereby, communications by the government to the people becoms empty rhetoric--see his promissory speeches--regulatory reflections of one-party Presidential Power. Already, the liberal, democrat brain-washed attitude engendered by the Omnipotent State has construed certain of the God's Ten Commandments as politically incorrect! The Supreme Court will prove to be commplicit in removing God entirely from American society.

        The direction of this increase in censorship is to make America a one-party system of government and therefore inevitably a dictatorship. To World-bankers money is the weapon of choice, the only way to rule out America's hedgemony of authority on the stage of a New World Order in which "global justice" will supercede Constitutional justice, the civilian trials of enemy GITMO combattants in NY, a politaical ploy, notwithstnding. Barack Obama has informed the world that GLOBAL JUSTICE is the desire of the American people. Such a monstrous fascistic lie ought not to go unopposed--though pleasing to globalist bankers (see European Bilderberg Group of 125 some-American Wall Street milti-billionaires). However, remember the cliche: the bigger the lie, the more readily it is accepted. The bigger the Govenmen in Washinon, the more credible and legtimate it appears to be as our true heritage of 1789. especially in view of the"updatling" of the US Constitution by the leftists in the Government, especially in the Supreme Court. Constraints on the Executive powers and rules for making change in the Constitution are anathema, a curse, to Barack Husein Obama, outlaw.

THE C RLSIS, b yCharles E.Miller

POSTSCRIPT. The Prewsident has demonsrated on a number of occasions--attacks on Israel, the Pam Am bombing, Kagtrina--his unwillingness to investigate the detaills of a tragedy, a world even that affects all Americans. This sort of high-minded negligence is proof of his inability to lead a free people. That sort of negligence lis both dangerous and naive, reprehensible in a sitting President, The Pan Am disaster was conceived and executed by a terrorist from another country. whom Obama dild not wsh to offend. Indeed, he is willing to sit down with dictator Almadinijad of Iran toconvince the despot that he ought not to attack Isreal. Yet he has already offended Israel as a legitiate nationbefore the Palestiians, who have never been a nation . This naivete of Barack Obama is both dangerous and misleading, both to those who still side with him and to others in the world whom we may rlightly consider to be our enemies...North Korea, China, Venezuela. What do they share with Preesident Obama but his Marxist ideology? His cowardce, naivete and incompetence, structured and driven by Marxism, is presenty dstroying his great nation. World peacein a world of tyrannical nations with evil desgns on weaker nations can be achieved and maintained not by words but by the show of power. That is what evil men understand. Satan understood Christ's rejecion of his temptations, not because Christ was a innocent and artliculate man, as He was, but because satan recognized the power of Almghty God in Christ. America's military power, combined with Presdent Reagan's strength of character and leadership, was a warning to Soviet Russia that bought about the dissolution of the Soviet Union and the demolition of the BerlinWall.

PROPAGANDIST OBAMA

Citizxen

The premise of this letter is that Barack Obama is a consummate propagandist and a sometimes liar. However, I would not write this letter if he had not offended me by his cocky manner, his preumptuous smile of victory, his gloating "victory party" with caviar and champaigne in a park, his egocentric acceptance of the Oval Room before the office is vacated, and his insincere embracement of all Americans. He comes. a fresh new product like a cleanser that people want to try. He reminds me of a side-show barker along the showway, a "snake-oil" salesman in his comportment. He comes with inexperience to take up the reins of this government requiring, as Senator McCain has said it, "on-the-job training." That is the pithy truth Nice guy and all, but...no thanks!;Propaganda can be defined in various ways Fundamentally, it is an attempt to manipulate another person(s), party or cause so as to achieve an objective that is hidden; Therefore propaganda involves deception to sway the emottions, and often indoctrination of the mind to achieve a policy end. It is psychological, emotional and controlling, like psychological warfare.Usually it is systematic and stems from policies of the perpetrator(s) ;

Propaganda lie #1 -- that the Iraqi war is a "dumb war" because it does not pursue Al Quaeda or Osama bin Ladin but invades a helpless country. Obama accepts some wars, like the Civil War, as honorable . His facts are wrong. Lincoln ordered war upon Fort Sumter primarily to "save the union," then to "abolish slavery." Check it out.

Propaganda lie #2--that Pakistan is available for invasion to hunt down Osama in the border mountains. This would destroy our friendship with Pakistan, an incursion without sufficient intelligence.

;Propaganda lie #3--that drillling offshore would corrupt the environment of its beauty, he thus captures the hearts of the most powerful lobby subgroup in American politics, the envionmentalists.

Propaganda lie # 4--that the surge is a failure, supported by the liberal media censorship of scenes on Baghdad streets, marketplaes, motor traffic, pedestrians conversing, and, in Afghanisan, the voting of the people, first time, for their own government, provisional though it may appear (I did see a few shots.). Camera coverage omits showing rebuilt schools by American soldiers, partial restoration of power, efforts to restore the infrastructure of Iraq. That censorship, implicitly supported by Obama, is a form of visual propaganda, it is a device to sway emotions, change attitudes and direct voters to his camp. It is political without any intercessory objections by Obama. I have neve, ever heard Oama commend the troops for their actual accompliishments in Iraq or in

afghanistan. The liberal press had "dumbed down the war."

Propaganda lie #5--he had only a casual acquaintance with bomber Ayers, when in fact he sat on boads to administer moneys, 800 thousand, to radicalize school kids in Chicago, the mentor for this taxpayer largesse being the unrepenten bomber and the Illinois taxpayers the source of the money.

Propaganda lie # 6--he disavows any sort of ideological connection to the Ayers bomber--which would infect his public image as a political purist--like using Americans to sociaize their own country, socialism being still a radical philosophy of state ownership of the means sof production, wich includes the fiancial institutions. Obama is nutured on the socialist notion of fiscal inequality, corrupt offspring of imperialist capitalism, and therefore must be addressed. This he will do...if in office.

Propaganda lie #7--the hate speech of his minister; Jeremy Wright   is not a part of his thinking...not that he also hates America, but that the America of the Civil War era still exists. He is ignorant, apparently, of the fact that Lincoln's first priority was not the eradication of slavery but the unification of America in the face of Secession.   Even today, Obama supports repartions, as if the blood shed in that horrible war were not enough. A pox on you,

Senaor.

Propaganda lie #8-- that he is a strong supporter of American labor and its rightful entitlements to the rewards thereof. However, he would spread the wealth about for the good of the people. The germinal; truth of Governor Palin's reembursements to the Alaskan people- was that their checks were their own money returned to them, not somebody else's extracted by fines, taxes and state regulations.

Propaganda lie # 9-- that Sen. McCain is a Bush clone. Senator McCain dilffers from President Bush in these (and in other) regards :
  --full closure of borders, including Canadian -- cessation of earmarks put into important bills, led by the "gang of three," Obama, Pelosi and Reid.--freeze on govt. spending for a year -elmination of useless agencies, duplication and of waste, which Bush has done virtually nothing about--saving vets, defense and vital needs agencies --curbing of 35,000 registered lobbyists in Washsington;--filling the still unfilled judgeships Bush has suggested , blocked by the Democrats in the Congress--repudiation of Bush philosophy of laisse faire, not by statism, not by a socialist regime but by stimilation of middle-class wealth through small business, investments--recovery of recsssion not by infusion of billions into banks and lenders, as Bush wants, but use of "bailout" money to purchase loans, at original value then promote renegotiation of said loans; A process, not a one time solution. McCain is far from being a George Bush II, a oft-repeated propaganda lie by Obama to justify CHANGE, not a program but a procedure.

Propaganda lie #10--that increased taxes on major companies in the US (to raise money for his entitlement programs, which include destruction of SS by inclusion of illegals and other non-citizens) willl help the US economic recovery. Actually, the excessive corporation tax has driven companys and jobs overseas, as informed people know. Who does he think he fools? By the way, the slaughtered 40 million babies were the next payor class of SS. Small wonder the lbierals want amnesty!;

Propaganda lie 11--small-town Americans are bitter, cling to their guns. That lie is a demonstration that he has not been brought up in America, is ignorant of its history, no doubt slanted by Harvard's professors of America's demise. His movie-star demeanor has won for him many fans...personable, smiling, playing always to the audience, an actor, a chamelleon in politics, changing his stance to accomomodate the crowd and to bring in votes. His rhetoric appeals to the emotions of the crowd, captives of psychological warfare, a sort of contemporary British Lord Ha Ha.

Propaganda lie #12--that he is for traditional marriage but supports gay marriage. He has never told the American people why he supports gay marriage. His propaganda sways emotions, manipulates the voters.

Propaganda lie #13--that slavery was not condemned nor freedom for blacks fully realized in the Civil Rights movement, nor in the Civil War. Yet anti-black animus can be eradicated with compensatory money, not with faith. He accepts Rev.Wright's position, secretly, I think, reinforced by his wife's comment about her late pride in this country.

Propaganda lie # 14 --that the bill to condemn botched abortions, introduced in the Illinois legislature, did not deserve a his support because....it would have offended the AMA, abortion clinics, Pro-choice US Supreme Court, the absortuaries, and feminist liberals. He is a panderer par excellence! He could not possibly have cut himself from their vote. No life for the trashed baby, but health care for living adults many of whom have trashed their health and expect the rest of society to pay for their unhealthy life styles. He is against the rescue of a discarded baby but for saving illegals, drug addicts, those who have paracticed unealthy lifestyles with a form of socialized medicine. fines attached to employers for non-conformity.When he government dictates condiisons for care, that is socialied medicine.

Propaganda lie #15--he has lied, and implicitly still does, that the surge was not fully effective. He has his reservations, despite Genl Petraeus' affirmation to the contrary

Propganda lie #16--America is not worth his exclusive loyalty but he must be loyal to the world as well, demonstrably toward those who hate us not for what we have but for who we are. I sense that neither he nor his wife feels that they are of the common people

;Propaganda lie #17--he lies, being deceived, that he can talk Ahmadinejad out of his plan to wipe Israel off the map and destroy America. Already radical Muslims and other would-be terrorists are trained in over 35 camps throughout the US, nominal Muslims enjoy perks in universities such as special prayer rooms and foot baths (Stanford being one) tolerate Islamic-dress days, recitation of the Koran by middle-choolers and even now a judge will welcome Sharia Law into his case profiles.Obama will trumpet for religious liberty such as will institute prayers in
schools, in the Congress, and on prominent places for display.
Watch!

Propaganda lie #18--the purpose and accomplishmens of US troops in Iraq are almost valueless, thus he voted to cut off their funds. Iraq is not worth any further investment of blood and money (like Iran, Venezuela, Syria, it is too small to worry about as a troublemaker).He is oblivious to the implications of political, as against military, withdrawal from Iraq. Remember: Obama is a citizen of the world and is impotent to respond, despite all other appearances. His cowardice will become evident.Just as he lacks the stuff to confront questions head on--a prevaricator, a rambling evader who prefers talk to action. discussion to direct answers. Let us discuss your hatred for the US. Let us talk about what you will not be allowed to do...such as bomb Pearl harbor. Two Japanese diplomats met in DC at the very moment of Pearl!

Propaanda lie #19--He will reduce taxes on 95 percent of Americans.Yet he will raise taxes on company and business payrolls, capital gains by investors and the thrifty, taxes on personal incomes. having voted to increase taxes 94 times while in the US Senate. He would win the votes of the middle-class yet, chamelon-like, increase taxes when and if he becoms President.   He would raise taxes...a plan he voted for this year 2008, that would raise taxes on Americans with incomes as small as $31.850! Obama wants it both ways. No taxes yet taxes.   His entitlement programs will require over one trillion new dollars to realize. A trillion is $1,000,000,000,000! Free money, instant wealth, no sacrifice, a handout from Uncle Sam, millions of you out there do not need all you earn. As a covert socialist he will define the word NEED, key to Marxian philosophy. A thousand of those somebodies may include you if you own a small business.

Propaganda lie #20--Natural gas is a Federal (not the people's) commodity. Although environmentally clean, it does not merit tax relief, being, indeed, the major energy source of the future and therefore taxable an controllable by the State. Do you not see how he would manipulate the energy sources, though he professes to espoue them all in order to produce the megabucks his CHANGE society will need.; He is a chameleon. But we keep that money at home. Sure.

Propaganda lie #21--his connection to the
voter/registration fraud of Acorn, already repcienf of thousands of taxpayer
dollas, is becming known. He lies to present the front of innocence--always
that--innocence---when his associations with Acorn go back to his lawyering
days.

Propaganda lie # 22-- being a friend of Louis Farakon, who
hates America with a passion, and JeremyWright, whose mansion makes him a
despicable hypocrite, Senator Obama's earlier associations plague his
candidacy. For he has not confronted each, publically, and told them
off. He is too cowardly to do so, leaning on "friendship" to dismiss the
corrupt relationships. I do not want that guy in charge of my country and
the troops in a world that has, by its own hatred of America, condemned us
already for being imperialists, war-mongers, racists, greedy capitalists and all
the other epithets which he would necessarily have to neutralize to be a
"citizen of the world." That center piece of his propaganda campaign will
do him in. It sounds"mod" and politically correct. But it reveals
his disaffection for the America of 219 years of struggle, bloodshed and
change. In my opinion, the mettle of the average-guy American is
somehow missing in his makeup. I see it, I sense it, I feel it. Maybe I'm too old to accept the
novelties of his candidacy, for which his adoring fans, illiterate of American history and
political philosophies, applaud (I may stand in contempt of court and do not regret that I
called the liberal members of the Supreme Court "swine in black robes." They support
murder in abortion clinics--choice (right to life, liberty). They suppo'covetous seizure by one
citizen of another's owned property for profit--Choice. (right to owernship, fruits of citizen's
labors) They support elimination of all expressions of faith in the public forum--choice
(freedom of religion).They support abominable homosexual marriage--choice (traditional
support of context of heterosexual family). You have my choice, Justices Stevens, Ginsberg,
Souter, et al. You have chosen when in doubt to abandon the Constitution, your sworn
oath to defend, and to opt for European decisions in the courts of France, Germany and
particularly the Netherlands. Barack Obama has been shaped by forces that are
largely alien to America. I think he lacks wisdom, fully-informed good judgement and the
experience of years. The complexity of this great nation and the formidible powers of darkess
that are arrayed against us are too enormous to entrust our country to the lonely judgement of
a virtual novice in these areas. A that desk in the oval office, his word will move
millions of lives, affecting them irrevocably, and billions in money, to whatever ends. A
forty-seven year old Senator with two years of "presemt"tenure in office, his emotions,
mental makeup visibly formed by questionble radicals in his past? I think not.

THE CRISIS by Charles E. Miller 10-21-08

POSTSCRI\PT: There is nothing clever, ystical orincredible about an avowed

Marxist lying to the commo people toadvance the tenets sof his radical ideology, all the while assu;ing that theyare too stupid tos ee through his lies especiallywhen they have lived free and almost Federalllyunfettered for over two hundred years. Obama takes Americans for fools lin his detestation of our free and open society. These lies are but the foudation to other lies to follow which will, inturn, reiforcehis lust for power and cotrol of a great nation. He thinks only of himself, henc his Messilanic complex, a pride not uncommon among the dictators of history. To ctch Obma lin alie, remember his broken promise that precedes the lie. Andnever for get that his cief purpose ilnthe spread of Federal power and the squandering of our wealth is Obama, himself. He yearns to be remembered as the Master Organizer, yet he lack the skill to organize a major industry and, instead, finds a certain perverse delight in trashing theirm as well as cotrolling the reainders of a once free industry, not the least of which are General Motors and Chrysler. .

BAIT AND SWITCH TO PASS OBAMACARE

Citizen.

You stick a gun in the face of the teller and order your pal to open the safe: That is a rule for robbery. The US Senate makes its own rules. Presently, the Amercn people are under the Senate gun, held by Pimp for poltical prostitution , Harry Reid. The Robbers are the liberal Democrats who intend to rob you, the investors in America, of their wealth and priceless liberty. That is a Senate rule--to trick you in order to rob you. Or, in political lingo, to exchange an acceptable law for a dubious law at the time of the House vote, that is to say--to corrupt the vote by this fraudulent malpractice of bait and swiltch.

But that rule has another appearance. The Healths Care bill that Conressman Reid has been "working on" will pass by reason of the operation of a house rule that is simply a bait- and-switch manipulation by Pimp Reid himself. He will hold the gun, a 2000 + page Socialist Healthcare bill that stands almost a foot high..he will get the Senate to adopt and "pass" this bill. Nobody has read it. It was not delivered until yesteday,Tuesday. Nobody understands it...lawyers. But the bill can be passed by reason of the Pimp's slight-of-hand that has become a rule for voting in the Senate (and in the House), a r ule by which a favoed bill is passed whilethererildes on it a controversialbill to theHouse. The House passes the favorablebill andbecause thecontroversialbill lis a "rider" onth former legislation,theHoue deems the controversial billtohave passed. That isfraud. Damn the rule of rider legislation...usually concerning innoculous bills of finance.

Senator Harry Reid is a faudulent operator, as are a majority of Democrats in the Senate. Bait and Swtch wil consist of this: Present a lesser bill that grants benefits to Veterans. Hooray! Then, remove that bill and substitute the healthcare bill without telling; the Senators. Thinking they are passing the veterans bill, they will vote to pass the bill on the table. Meantime, Speaker Harry Reid has substitued the healthcare monster for the vets bill and the vote is to pass the bill before the Senate. The bill that has pased is replaced by the bill that is in danger of failing. It will pass readily. by reason of he fraud just committed by Harry Reid on the Senate and on the people of this great land. Baited by the Veterans billl, the House passes the controversail bill. Noboby, but nobody, in the Senate will have the slightest sound knowledge and understanding of the Reid bill. Is that procedure, if not deceit, fraud and dishonesty, a form of political madness that we will be paying for for generations? I that despicable deceit is abuse of power. Is that not malfeasance under the aw, the holdup robbey, Senate rule not withstanding. If I blindfolded a man and told him to sign a conract for the sale of his property, took his money and then called the deal honest and law-abiding, that would be a felony or at least a malfeasance, a fraud on my part.

The Congress, run by Democats, has turned into a rotten piece of political junk who would even consider this piece of legalistic crap. The fraud of bait and switch will occcur, count on it. Senators who vote for this bill, after the bait and swich fraud, are verifiablyparticipats lin a dishonest operation of the Congress. For they hve disarmed both their weaker colleagues and duped the American people. In doing so, they steal from the nation its history of freedom and opportunity and enterprise by stuffing Obamacare down the people's throats and commanding their silence or the imposition of heavy fines as penalties. The Congess has turned into a gargantuan charlatan that threatens to take over the; preservation of our freedoms. The pipsqueek cowardly media are greatly to blame for this internal destruction of America.

Article I, Section 8 of the US Constitution states: "The Congress shall have the power...to make all laws which shall be necessary and proper for carryng into Execution the foregoing Powers, and all their Powers vested for the Constitution in the Government of the United States, or in any Department or Officer thereof."

The Senate, like the House, makes its own rules. Bait and swilch is a rule of the senate . It has been done before. (What voters knew that?) It will be done with the healthcare bill, initiated by Harry Reid, the cynical pimp for corrupted democrat politicians who, prostituting their office of trust, will vote to pass the Senate Bill without having read it or disclussed it or amended it. Congressman Harry Reid thinks the bill is a done deal, and this monster will pass, to the delight of that smiling , arrogant socialist deceiver in the white house and all the other crooks who mitigate the anxiety of trial lawyers, cronies, special interests and Federal unions, by their cooperating votes. It's ready to cast off...thus who doubts what I am saying?

That abuse of power, that fraudulent switcharoo of bills is a rule, like the rule for a bank holdup I just cited. The smiling face behind the gun will be Obama, the crook who robs this nation of a fundamental industy, its health care enterprises. He and his cohorts are the safe robbers. We are supposed to remain mute, confined to our dreams of past glory, in order to permit this sleuth for degeneracy, Barack; Hussein Obama and his pirates rob the people of one sixth of the GNP, and indebt the taxpayers not with 787plus billions of baillout money, but one and one third thrillions in a debt passed along to three, four generations.

Senator Harry Reid is about tovbegin his holdup rule forrobbing the people of their freedom ofchice in halth care. The Pirates in the Senate stand ready to vote blind, without understandkilng, comp[ehension, debvate, opporition...just dumb silence ofvrutes...andcrooks who want what they ;want, money and power. Money is the name of this bill. Big, big Money from th safe of the American tasxpayers, the crooiks who swirl the safe nobe and scoop out the moeny are our alleged represetatives in both Houses.

I told you so. I knew I knew that the House would use the healthcare bill as a rider on ...I thought then...on TARP. Like the Senate plans to do, t hey passed it with mindless concurrence. These monsters of confusion are vulnerble to instant Washington spin.

Mindless crooks, Liberal Senators are whoremongers for power and money and control of the people. And Harry Reid is about to pull his bait-and-switch act this week-end. A Senate vote without knowledge is tyranny over the people. One talk-show host said that Senator Harry Reid should be run out of Washington, DC on a rail, literally. I agree. And those who vote for his monstlrosity of legalese and confusion and people-control should be driven from their desks into the yard withl ;a shotgun at their backs, for they are robbing the people of their most priceless possession, their liberty of free choice in an area that affects them so intimaltely and dramatically and permanently--their health care.

I warn you: you will never reverse this vote for such a draconian change that robs Americans of the finest health care in the world. Neve, ever. You will never expunge its cruel demands for inferior care, its interminable waiting, its crushing taxes and its rationing ir lis rationing for early death and care-denial.

The bills, both House and Senate are evil. They reintrodces the slavery of cost-effectiveness of a person's medical care, built into the bill. Are you worth your hire to pick cotton in Islander Obama's cotton field. Your only value to determine your medical care is your monetary value to the State. The State. The State is almighty god--the Central Government run by plutocrat socialists, led by Obama. Your worth is monetary, no more, to determine your worthiness for care and in many cases your right to life..

How do I know. By comparisons of centralized care with individual-choice care and, most apparently, by the application of Senate malfeasance viz a viz Senator Harry Reid's fraululent trickery that demolishes our present health-care system. Harry Reid and the democrat crook-pracitioners in the Senate, the safe-crackers, lack character. They are corrupt.

The demons of hell have been waiting a long time to destroy America. It is about to happen. For, with the control of the healthcare industry, the insurance industry,the car industry, the banks and the health-care industry, little more remains to control but the regulation t of the religion (industry?)

I warn you, if you pass this bill, you will run to daddy in Washington for almost everthing, including pemission to go out and play, With jealous eyes you will regard the savings of those who by their private means, diligence and chararacter did not succumb to the blandishments of Senator Harry Reid and the Democrat pirate-whores in Congress. Damn the veterans, damn the American people in their dumb "leadership" expectations.

THE CRISIS, by Charles E. Miller

POSTSCRIPT: The presence of outlawry in practice is pelucidlyvisible to thinking Americans. The Cjharlatanliberals linthe Senate know how toplay the game of political leverage and well-connected li;nfluence. The scenarios sketched in her are so devious limnc haracgter as to rebukethe founders bytheir fraud. Once an elected offlicil tarts downsthe road of deceptinand correupt dealings, he isalmost certailn not toturnback. Senator

Reild issuch a manand becaue of his posslition as Senate Seaker, lisils also a dangero;us man whos elinfluence canbe expunged, or a least lessened, only by theelection process. He represents the nature and visionofthe present administrtion, ongong enlargement oftheFederalgovernmentandundeniable corruptin both visible and in secret. It isthelatter thecitizenshoudlfear more than theslims apparent onthe dailystage of Washington politics. Beward of thesecfet government, nttheleast ofwhichare the unconstitutionalczars. Watch and reject....

FEDERAL HEALTHCARE JURISDICTION `
UNCONSTITUTIONAL

Citizen.

We are "fortunate" to have Constitutional lawyers in the House who are competent to decide issues within their jurisdiction. What category of jurisdiction, Mme. Speaker? Jurisdiction over persons, subject matter, Federal and State both original and pending? Which does the good dame mean?

The blank-cheque statement is worthless before the oath to support and defend the Constitution of the United States. Under Articie I, Section 8, clause 18, the Congress has the power "to make all Laws whch shall be necessary and proper for carrying into Execution the foregoing Powers and all other Powers vested by this Constitution in the Governmen of the United States or in any Department or Officer thereof."

Question: Where is the implication or command or constraint on liberty of advice appertaining to the healthcare welfare of the entire people either denoted, suggested, demanded or implied in the a;bove clause of the Constitution? I an a literate person, yet I cannot find that supervening and all-inclusive authoritygilven to the Federal Goernment to swab my throat or amputate my leg or conduct my heart surgery.

Therefore, the Government's command that I and other citizens take out health insurance--whether mandated from both houses or from one only--defies logic, reason and common sense as improper, unlawful and un-Constitutional. The Constitutional jurisdicion of said Powers does not empower either Congressmen or Senators to invent a supra-power not implied or granted by Article I, Sec 8, clause 18.

You Congressmen covet the power to control what is most vital and sensitive to the people--their personal health. You criminalize non-compliance by your denial of free choice, and your threats of imprisonment. What if the youthful citizen cannot afford either the $3,800 fine or the cost of a jail term and an additional fine? You would impose medicare edits that are injurious and destuctive to freedom in America. Your lust for oligarchial command that we shall to your will and judgement conform is evident in the health-care bill you present.

You do not understand it, nor will the people. Yet you thrust upon 300 million individuals the contempt for our present system, which we find adequate, all the while ensconcing your colleagues-in-law--the trial lawyers--in readiness to debase the

Constitution, defraud the people of the truth about our care, and crush the life from the general citizenry with court penalties based on your ill-gotten notions of justice. You are convinced that any crappy law you shall inven is protected by the jusice of a virtuous Fedeal Government In short, you plan to encourage trial lawyers to grow fat upon the lives of medical practitioners, while you, like buzzards, will never be satisfied. This curse of darkness you intend o visit upon the American people with your Obamacare, You soulless giants of disesteem and pigmy intellect, Reid, Pelosi and radical leftists in both Houses of the Congress. You assume a status of superior intelligence that is demonstrated neither by your words nor by your actions. Your dull, small minds and corrupt intentions will destroy the gifted in this great Constitutional Republic. You radical leftists in the Congress and in the Administration are a den of vipers!

Those laws, by the way, ladies and gentlemen of the Congress, were made solely for the proteciton of the people from the oppressive, destructive and unlawful use of power by officials in office, the which you represent. You are certainly not the British Parliament of 1776. The US Constitution was not constructed for the benefit and aggrandizement of sitting elected officials or grasping bureaucrats, howsoever well intentioned. I am a student of men as well as of the Constitution. l am certainly not your huckleberry.

What are those foregoing Powers and all other Powers vested by this Constitution in the Government of the United States or in any Department or officer thereof? Do they suggest that Congreessmen are not to trust the people? Do those powers mock over two hunded years of our brilliant history of struggle and enterprise and freedom? Do such allege outside-the-law inventions cancel out pleadings by the opposition, namely, that the health care (and other monsterous legislation) is destructive to this nation? Indeed, do your privae practices as lawyers intrude upon your good judgement as elected officials? We, the people, are not your clients. That attitude , I suspec, is partly the case. We will, in fact, tell you arrogant sheisters how to run your office, and if you find this depresses your egomania and infringes upon your will to control the people, then get out and good riddance. Goback to your private kingoms of law practice. More civic-worthy men and women will replace you. Humility ia not your Zeitgeist.

To Mme Pelosi I say that empowerments of "original" and/or of "pendant" jurisdictional control by House members, regardless of their legal education, is worthless, irrelevant and unlawful. They are gratuitous emoluemnts of her--and Senator Reid's--radical chosing. The Speaker of the House does not possess that "original" power, especially when standing before the last clause quoted above. She has not the authority to concockt a power and then to bestow that power upon any Congresman or Congresswoman, like a royal Madam, Queen of the realm. She thereby emboldens them with a jurisdictional aura they do not possess in generality. For the Constitution is very speclific in its grant to Congress of Parliamentary discretion to make any law lawful. (Parliment tried that with the Stamp Tax, the flint that ignited the powder of our Revolution. Brittons against Brittons.)

It was deliberately designed so in order that the people, fugitives from similar oppressive mercenaries in Europe, might live in freedom, the freedom to make their own choices about what is most intimate to them, their medical care. Have you ever heard of the plague, the black death, and the causal lack of standards of sanitation and cleanliness, about medically-induced bleeding to cure a disease, about phoney medicines called "elixirs of healing," about hypnosis healing, abouit healing magic, charlatans of medicine, and taking the cure in waters, and more ? Obamacare would return to this country some of these delusions of good medical care. Like phoney medications, quackery treatment and the black art of political persuasion that Uncle Sam is taking care of you and your children. The rdical elitists inWashingtontake you for dumb and ignorant idiots. Beling power-gabbing charlatans , they are convilnced that they are right inthis magter of your halthcare. They are delusional and idolatrous of their power, beyond the constraints of Constitutional law.

Trusting in God as they did for their welfare and their very survival, that included good health, theyfled old vassal-state Europe. Imitating the prince of deception, our President would turn you to imitate old Europe by his collaborationist (leftists in Congress) elimination of enlightened medicine in the US.

Furthermore, we who will be the alleged "beneficiaries of said bestowal have a right to reject that power because we are neither subjects of the Obama crown, nor are we vassals of the Federal Governmen-State. If we do so, let it be said that we --not all conservatives, by the way--rebel with intelligence and comprehension. We are citizens under the laws of the land. No Congressperson has an INHERENT right to override the circumscribed power of his his or her office in order to effect a law, a change in a law, a provision added to a law, a consequence of a law, an re-interpretation of a law, a personal application of a law, a new law without debate, discussion or a vote of the House. A seat in the Congress is not the same venue as member-management of a law firm. We are not your clients, you arrogant lawyer who intend to radicalize our democracy with some sort of sis-boom-bah Marxist cant of medical care! Keep in mind that you are our servants...servants of the people. If that galls you, find another job or go back to your law practice. You are adept at taking a side, one or the other, the prosecxution or the defense. But you are unsuited by your experience to ascertain, with honesty, probity and discernment, the common-sense aspects of a medical problem. You are therefore unsuited to medically diagnose and treat an entire nation of the hurt, sick and disabled. That is what your Obamacare bill implies. You assue a cogent relationship to medical science.

Poitical skimmer Mme. Pelosi's attempt to empower Constitutional lawyers in the House (Reid in the Senate) with non-existent power, for to to impose a presently moot law without its formal introducion is illegal and unlawful. That breech of existent statutes will come to light eventually. Her intent is not to urge "Constitutional lawyers" to observe proposals in their respective committees but, instead, to propose, and essentially to promise, laws which will override the inherent democratic perspectives of relevance, balance of opinion, her proposal of legislation being effecitve by virtue of the lawyers's expeience and training. It is not Madam Speaker Pelosi's office to cause a possible law to conform to the wishes of a radical leftist president--to the prejudice of the will of the people, no matter how celestial the law. One cannot ethically talk about Obamacare as if it were already the law and needed but brush-up touches to improve upon it. That spin is unethical deception and it is intellectually dishonest.

The following are the Constitutionally authorized venues of power-to-control for Constitutional lawyers, and others in both Houses.

Taxes, duties, excxises
defense
regulate commerce
naturalization
coin money
fight counterfeiting
disclose and fight piracies
war and supporting legislation
estabilsh a amilitia
control of DC
HEALTH CARE FOR THE PEOPLE...? Is that empowerment actually there?
No. not without a Constitutional Amendment! The people have a right to disobey the
Federal Government in this connection.

I see no specific law that empowers the Congress to demand that the people sign
up for, accept Federdal control of, bear the cost and the regulations of, or conform to threats
of imprisonment and fines thereof, or subject themseles to regulations imposed by the
Congress for the mangemen and acceptance of medical care for their personal health. Pelosi
and the other leftist liberals who plan to force the people , like British subjects of the king,
not citizens of a Constitutional Republic, to bend their knees to the Federal law of
Obamacare. The Leftists are asking for trouble from the people. Ameicans are not prepared
to abandon their great heritage like cowards in the face of danger. This is especially true
when we realize tht Pelosi, Reid, and other far-left liberals skim money from bills into their
personal accounts, buy the votes of Congressmen who want to pinch and sniff at a law, and
fawn upon lobbyists who gamble fortunes to block the will of the people. What are you
running there in Washington, you Poltroons of spending graft and chicanery? You betray
the people in your will to follow that European Fraud in the White House. I think it was
C.S. Lewis who decried your sort as "men without chests."

THE CRISIS, by Charles E. Milller

POSTSCRO[T" Never lin our wo hundred andthirteen years of history has
anylaw portended tograb one seventy ofthe nation's economy.Bythis law, doctors, nurses,
entire hosptals, medical insuranceocompanieswill fall under ederal,distant control. The
individuals medical problems willbe assessed and treatment mandagted byabsent docgtors
and politicians in Washington. Thebill will not onlybe extremelycostlybut
precariouslydangerousto theetire profession, especiallytopatlients whose medilcalcondition
cannot possiblyb e diagnosed by electronics from adistance of a few iles to thespan of the
nation. Obamacare, as it is called, is so unconstiltutional that any entities, companies,
persons, groups, organizations, entire states have reqiested waivers from the bill's onerous
provisions. Te bill is a patent act of arrogant outlawry promoted by leftists in the
Administration, liberals in the Congress, shady support groups and money. Obamacare is an
act of political outlawry that will never be accepted by a free people.

ILLITERACY IN AMERICA

Citizen.

I've just finished a re-reading Jonathan Kozol's excellent book "Illiteeate America." Illiteracy in this country is a social as well as a political and economic problem.

Obama...and Bush...have declned to close the borders, The cocky "moat with allegators" comment by Obama was the stupid admission of that fact, and of his intent NOT to close the borders, a give-away of his sinister design for this nation's future, a dumbed-down America. A dumbed-down America, shorn of skepticism and the ability to think as indiduals is an easy to control America. The loss of cognition--the capacity to reason, absorb information and analyze tha;t information is the way to subjection.--a humbled America. A Godless America, by demigogic Preacher Wrights anti-Biblical standards.

What is happening is a deliberate attempt by Obama and his leftist corrupters to increase America's illiteracy, starting in the schools. ?Their rant to ilmprove the classroom performance of our schoolchildren is so much political rant. Obama had to appease e the poeerful Teachers Unions who support him, Had the summons come from the PTA would have thought differently.

To be sure, some teachers are more effective than others in their work; it has always been so. It is more apparent nowadays because the The President's persuasion by and agreeing with his Marxist advisors in the Administration endorses illiteracy in America, while pounding their blockheads for more money for the teachers and removing the ineffective ones. That is a scam. Remove the illegals lin elemenary schools, reduce class size, put teaching ino the hands soflocal schools , principals and parent communities. The NEA is a bureau of political garbage whose only connection to eucation is as a yea-sayer.to the Marxist left. We all know that when a dictator wants to control a country, he begins with the young.

The problmem is oversize classrooms stuffed with illegals who do not speak Englishs and do not intend to do so. They collect as illegals on the school grounds. They do not intermingle, they; continue to raise the class sizes in America's schools. Good teachers have had to dumb down their instruction to try to reach all the students, the illegals and the non-productive kids.

The leftist scum in Washington blame the teachers, the lack of money, the ineptitude of the legal citizen students. Whereas the problem is the ongoing dumbing down of the legitimate students who speak English and are alredy integrated with out culture.

Why increase the iliteracy in America? Is that not a unconslcioanbly stupid idea. It is, but remember, Obama loved the dictators of the world, embraced them and scorned our friends. Dictators thrive on Illiteracy. They exist and contol an entire nation because illiterate people cannot read ballots, as in America, cannot write letters of protest as in America, cannot, as illiterates, read the newspapers, as in America, are propaganized as illiterates by TV liberals, as in America. Putting these ineptitudes together, Barack Obama can better control the direction to "transform America. " An illiterate America is a vulnerable America, without the anti-biotic of literacy to resist evil, commend virtue, trust the reliable and condemn the criminal...by the use of their informed intelligences gotten though literate communication--words. cognition. informed reasoning.

Not only are iliterates easily misled. cannot read or write, are swayed by friends and polticians, do not vote except when the candidate is different in color or politics. They often suspect trickery by the opposition. They cannot read candidate arguments or voting-booth ballots.

Illiteracy will bring America down/ Illiteracy is engendered and encouraged by open borders, mocked by that White House jerk's response of "moats with allegators." He gave himself away. His intentions are crystal clear...no borders (therefore no sovereignty for the US).

We do not, have never frightened legitimate emmigrants from entering the US. Because Barack Obama is an outlaw, he does not comprehend that reality. He pretends that we native citizens want to keep out newcomers. Checkmate.

He ignores the illegitimacy of fence-crossers. He ignores the need for entry rules, legitimate entries with his stupid crack, typical of a hidden Muslim, He scorns our efforts to seal the borders. He claims to want to fix the deterioration of America's classrooms... due to size increased by illegals... and to do so with money and the elimination of some teachers...all without fixing major problem of teachers having to address overcrowding by Illegals. Theanswer: get rid of "incompetent " teachers, i.e. non-bilingual teachers! He strikes first at the teachers instead of at his policy of open borders and the effects thereof on our schools.

He is devious, shrewd in a dumb sort of way, repeatedly practicing outlawry. Illegals are his future voters. His joke is an admission that we should keep the borders open. Fear to cross? Laughable!

Remember: An illiterate people (in 1985, 60 + million by Kozol's estimate), enough to determine the vote are easily misled, propagadized, brainwashed and changed from citizens into subjects. AN ILLITERATE AMERICA IS A TRANSFORMED AMERICA...INTO A THIRD-WORLD SOCIALIST STATE. When and if that should happen, we will never again back our lost inividual liberties ...ever...ever. Some may try with comic books--as by Mexico. We will only read--we who can read-- about what life was like when men were free . Our tyrant and Master will shed crocodile tears. You illiterates, without knowledge, will applaud his compassion. You will thank him for "his truth," and return to your play.

THE CRISIS, by Charles E. Miler 5-21-11

POSTSCRIPT: You who lack a great vocabulary, remember those weekly word-lists of 20 words per list that your 11th-grade teacher "forced on" you? Eh? (if you did not drop out of high school and are now a semi-literate) Read a good book. Try the Bible, as in Puritan days. Look up each word and use it in a sentence.

Paper due Friday. 20 words per list, that you scorned. to learn. Tough anagrams, indolent smartie! Suffer...or change your attitude toward increasing your linguistilc ability...in Enlish. Don't omit the sentence work! Strange words are more likely to stick in your memory that way. You prefer slang sometimes; purchase a slang dictionary for American English! Make up your own list of words you do not know , become familiar with the English dictionary, and use each word in a sentence. Be your own teacher. Yea! And don't be afraid of using your new words in fromt of your dumbed-down friends. Then find new friends. If you have tried yet occasionally grope for a word, you have my honest empathy. The human language is Man's highest civilized achievement! Do not let the Washington leftist, Marxist Socialist bastards convert us into a third-rate, dumed down person in nation of illiterates or we are lost...forever...as a free people!

`` Politicians will pussh the sciences as subject for empasis ilnthe grades, whereas competency in the English langluagbe is a firstrequissite for competent job formation a nd enlightened ciltizenship. What lis missing is abroad perspective of what shouldbe achieved bystudents lin elementary andsecondaryschools: a literate use of thecommon tongue,in America iltisEnglish. The carve of The Outlaw isto ontrol the study aterialsby suggestions that suindi ate lindoctrinatio for the useoftheState rather than in the private sector.